ROMAN SOCIAL IMAGINARIES

LANGUAGE AND THOUGHT IN CONTEXTS OF EMPIRE

THE ROBSON CLASSICAL LECTURES

William S. Anderson, *Barbarian Play: Plautus' Roman Comedy*, 1993

Niall Rudd, *The Classical Tradition in Operation*, 1994

Alexander Dalzell, *The Criticism of Didactic Poetry*, 1996

M. Owen Lee, *The Olive-Tree Bed and Other Quests*, 1997

David Konstan, *The Emotions of the Ancient Greeks*, 2001

Elaine Fantham, *Latin Poets and Italian Gods*, 2003

Brent D. Shaw, *Bringing in the Sheaves: Economy and Metaphor in the Roman World*, 2008

Clifford Ando, *Roman Social Imaginaries: Language and Thought in Contexts of Empire*, 2012

CLIFFORD ANDO

Roman Social Imaginaries

Language and Thought in Contexts of Empire

UNIVERSITY OF TORONTO PRESS
Toronto Buffalo London

Toronto Buffalo London
www.utppublishing.com

ISBN 978-1-4426-5017-6

Library and Archives Canada Cataloguing in Publication

Ando, Clifford, 1969–, author
Roman social imaginaries : language and thought in contexts of empire / Clifford Ando.

(Robson classical lectures)
Includes bibliographical references and index.
ISBN 978-1-4426-5017-6 (bound)

1. Rome – Languages – Political aspects. 2. Latin language – Rome. 3. Roman law – Language. 4. Cognitive grammar. 5. Rome – History – Empire, 30 B.C.–284 A.D. I. Title. II. Series: Robson classical lectures

P119.32.R64A54 2015 306.44'093763 C2015-900126-9

University of Toronto Press acknowledges the financial assistance to its publishing program of the Canada Council for the Arts and the Ontario Arts Council, an agency of the Government of Ontario.

University of Toronto Press acknowledges the financial support of the Government of Canada through the Canada Book Fund for its publishing activities.

Contents

Acknowledgments

This book was written in response to an invitation to deliver the Robson Classical Lectures at Victoria University at the University of Toronto in 2012. The material and intellectual hospitality that I received during my visit was exemplary, and I owe thanks for questions and conversation to more members of that community than I can name. But I owe special debts to Alison Keith, who issued the invitation, and Jonathan Edmondson of York University, my former chair. Their friendship, and indeed the example of their personal and scholarly conduct, sustained me in my first years in the profession and have accompanied me ever since.

The material in this book was discussed in seminars at Columbia University, the Institut National de l'Histoire de l'Art in Paris, the University of Chicago, the University of Michigan, and the University of Pisa. To the audiences on those occasions, my thanks. The final preparation of this manuscript took place at the Notre Dame Institute for Advanced Study, and I am grateful to the Institute for its hospitality.

In addition to two anonymous readers for the Press, several friends read the book in manuscript: Kathy Eden, David Grewal, Joshua Katz, Bruce Lincoln, and John Weisweiler. It is all too easy in scholarly life to take the giving of learning, time, and acumen for granted. I hope the result repays in some small way their extraordinary generosity. For answers to questions and help with bibliography, I am also indebted to Guy Bradley, Michael Fronda, Sebastian Matzner, and Michael Snowden.

This book would not exist – it would be so different as to be another book altogether, as I would be a different person – had I not had as interlocutors all these years Ruth Abbey and Sabine MacCormack. Sabine died just before the lectures were drafted, and yet all who knew her will recognize the meaning of my claim that she was and remains my companion in reflection, however far away.

And then there is Theodore, who grows and grows. I wake up early to make him coffee, and it is never a chore.

Abbreviations and a Note on Translations

Abbreviations

AÉ	*L'Année Épigraphique*
ARS	A.C. Johnson, P.R. Coleman-Norton, and F.C. Bourne. *Ancient Roman Statutes*. Austin: University of Texas Press, 1961.
CIL	*Corpus Inscriptionum Latinarum*
Dig.	A. Watson, ed. *The Digest of Justinian*. 4 volumes. Philadelphia: The University of Pennsylvania Press, 1985.
FIRA	S. Riccobono, ed. *Fontes Iuris Romani Antejustiniani*. 3 volumes. Florence: Barbèra, 1941.
FRHist	T.J. Cornell, ed. *The Fragments of the Roman Historians*. 3 volumes. Oxford: Oxford University Press, 2013.
Lenel	O. Lenel. *Palingenesia Iuris Civilis*. First edition Leipzig 1889. Reprinted with a supplement by Lorenz E. Sierl, 1960. Aalen: Scientia Verlag, 2000.
OLD	P.G.W. Glare, ed. *Oxford Latin Dictionary*. Oxford: Clarendon Press, 1982.
RE	*Realencyclopädie der classischen Altertumswissenschaft*
TLL	*Thesaurus linguae latinae*

A Note on Translations

Where I have used or adapted a published translation, the debt is acknowledged in the citation. An exception to this rule is the collective translation of Justinian's Digest edited by Alan Watson, on which I have drawn without noting the individual translator responsible for the book in question.

ROMAN SOCIAL IMAGINARIES

INTRODUCTION

Roman Social Imaginaries

This book seeks to initiate two conversations about Roman antiquity, one of which might be described as substantive, the other as concerning method. The two are complexly intertwined. At a substantive level, the chapters focus on a set of topics – "Belonging," "Cognition," and "The Ontology of the Social" – as well as a series of subsidiary issues – political and ethnic identity, territoriality, geographic contiguity and conceptual affinity, consent and normativity, materiality and metaphysics – that stand in oblique relation to the explicit concerns of Roman political and legal thought, but which have been, and are today, central to social and political theory.

At the level of method, my concern lies not with the propositional content of some Roman social theory, but with the archetypal concepts and habits of mind that endowed that propositional content with structure and meaning, conditioned and shaped its articulation, and guided and constrained its development. Above all, I am interested in patterns of metaphor, metonymy, analogy, and ideation – those features of language that serve in particular traditions within cognitive linguistics to map fundamental structures of thought, specific to particularized linguistic and discursive systems.[1] Where Roman legal and political argument is concerned, it was these operations that simultaneously acknowledged and expanded the limits of their language and the conceptual and taxonomic apparatus to which that language gave voice and gives access. The focus of this book is therefore not simply on what Romans understood themselves to be saying and thinking, but also on how they thought, and further, upon the constraints, both positive and negative, placed upon what they thought by how they thought.

Much might be embraced within such a program. One might proceed in a Lakoffian fashion and study the lexical apparatus employed in Latin to describe intellection – the use of verbs of sense-perception to describe understanding ("I see what you mean"), and the privilege thereby granted to sight, which finds echoes in the moral valuation accorded to light and dark, and so forth. From an almost infinite range of possible topics, I have selected material with a particular goal in mind, namely, to bring to light and to explore structures of thought that shaped and sustained the Roman empire as a political form: presuppositions in regard to political belonging – and identity more broadly – that undergirded a liberal, contractarian position in regard to immigration and manumission; patterns in ideation and argument that allowed a Latinate legal system to regulate the affairs of non-Latinate populations, dwelling in material and ecological conditions unimagined and perhaps unimaginable in the context of the law's original production; habits of abstraction that permitted the reduplication of institutional structures across a heterogeneous landscape; and understandings of the social that sustained policies of pluralism in the domains of religion and law.

The title of this book pays homage to Charles Taylor's *Modern Social Imaginaries*, with which it shares certain historical and interpretive ambitions but from which it differs crucially in method (as well as historical period). Some explanation of how this is so might serve to clarify what is at stake in this project. Taylor describes the object of his inquiry as "the background understanding behind practice" (25) or, alternatively, the "common understanding that makes possible common practices and a widely shared sense of legitimacy" (23).[2] But where Taylor extracts propositional claims from philosophical and political literatures, sufficiently abstracted from their historical and linguistic context so as to enable an aggregated portrait of some modern (Western) thought-world, I study patterns of figuration, comparison, and ideation within a specific linguistic system. My notion of background or common understanding thus embraces those aspects of language that might truly be said to lie in the background, susceptible of description as non-propositional operations through which other, properly propositional material is given voice.[3]

But while metonymic reach and the scope of analogical elaboration are not often at the forefront of conscious awareness and can legitimately be described as both background and shared, I focus on them precisely because they are themselves the product of historical developments (language coming to say that which we call upon it to do) and because their conventional and contingent limitations in turn shape what a language can say and a speaker can think at any given moment. What is more, the great historical sweep of the Latin language allows one to witness the birth, development, and naturalization (or death, if you will) of specific figures, or changes in the metonymic reach of certain clusters, and invites thereby historical reflection on the imbrication of linguistic–cognitive shift and contextual change. To return to the point above, it is therefore the necessary and essential role of figurative language in the construction of propositional content that makes the substantive and methodological aspects of this project truly intertwined.

This book should also be read as inspired by, and responding to, two further works: Michel Foucault's *The Order of Things* and John Pocock's *The Machiavellian Moment*.[4] As regards Foucault, Roman studies has produced only tentative gestures towards an inquiry into the distinctive flavour of a Roman ordering of the world, one which respects the enormous prestige they accorded, and influence they granted, to the discipline and language of the law.[5] This study suggests one route such an inquiry might take. Where Pocock is concerned, chapter 3 of this work can be read as taking up his arguments about the role of historicism and historical self-awareness, of temporality and finitude, in the Atlantic republican tradition. This work locates the roots of these phenomena in the remarkable historicism of Roman social thought. The work required to explain the passage of these distinctive ways of being and reflecting from the one context to the other, and the teasing out of the implications of this argument for Pocock's achievement, must however be postponed to another day.

Classical studies more generally, and even classical history narrowly construed, are disciplines with deep roots in philology. This project therefore exists in a relation of affinity to a number of lexical studies: Jean Béranger's remarkable inquiries into the languages of politics in the imperial period, for example, or John Richardson's essay on the emergence of a concept of empire, or Myles Lavan's recent book on metaphorical accounts of social relations between Romans and others in the early empire, to name only a few of which I am particularly fond.[6] To my mind, these works recuperate and study a vocabulary, rather than a grammar, of Roman thought.[7] This project, by contrast, concerns itself with the problem of cognition in the context of empire, in which a singular linguistic and discursive system is brought through political action into contact with, and then made to regulate, human societies in every way removed from the conditions in which that system had come into being. Political and practical realities can always race beyond a given culture's ontological commitments and the metaphorical apparatus available to render them meaningful, and so they did in the case of Rome. The problem of materiality as a component of political belonging – of belonging to the soil on which one was born and dwells – is a case in point. At the same time, the demands of empire nurtured and encouraged the creative potential of humans as linguistic and self-interpretive beings, and so new languages were born, by which the emergent realities of the high Roman empire might be described using language of absolute familiarity as nonetheless extraordinarily different.

This book is an effort to explain how that story might be told, by modelling three studies on Latin as a language of law and empire.

CHAPTER ONE

Belonging

Miserable oppression was the lot of the Carthaginians, who had accepted the Roman peace with the provision that they could keep their life, their city and their substance. For they understood by the city its buildings, for which sense the Latin word is *urbs*; but the Romans had used the word *civitas*, which means the community of citizens.

– Giambattista Vico[1]

1. I start with the term *civitas*, an abstraction from *civis*, meaning "citizen." The primary meaning of *civitas* is therefore "citizenship," the quality or property that makes someone a citizen and which all citizens share.

By metonymies standard already in the classical period *civitas* could also mean both "citizen body" and "city," which is to say, it might be synonymous with *populus* and *urbs* ("people" or "citizen body" and "city" or "conurbation"). I will take up the implications of the synonymity between *civitas*-as-citizenship and *civitas*-as-community at greater length in the next chapter and conclusion. At present, I want to pursue the interrelationship between the implicit understanding of how political communities are to be defined and the presuppositions regarding territoriality and materiality that inhere in Roman thinking about political belonging in the classical period. As we shall see, the material and sociological conditions of Roman political discourse underwent substantial change in the high and late empire, and those changes placed considerable strain upon those presuppositions.

That strain is visible not least in the gradual dissolving of the associative network interanimated by the term *civitas* in the classical period – though I will close with some remarks on the resilience of those commitments and the lexical apparatus through which they were articulated.[2]

First, however, we must come to grips with a latent meaning of *civitas* not treated in standard lexica, namely, *civitas* as territory of a political community. Consider, for example, three different ways of talking about jurisdiction.[3] The first appears in Cicero's description of the legal landscape of Roman Sicily:

Siculi hoc iure sunt ut, quod civis cum cive agat, domi certet suis legibus, quod Siculus cum Siculo non eiusdem civitatis, ut de eo praetor iudices ex P. Rupili decreto, quod is de decem legatorum sententia statuit, quam illi legem Rupiliam vocant, sortiatur. Quod privatus a populo petit aut populus a privato, senatus ex aliqua civitate qui iudicet datur, cum alternae civitates reiectae sunt; quod civis Romanus a Siculo petit, Siculus iudex, quod Siculus a civi Romano, civis Romanus datur; ceterarum rerum selecti iudices ex conventu civium Romanorum proponi solent. (Cicero *Verr.* 2.2.32)

The Sicilians are subjects of law as follows: actions of a citizen with a fellow citizen are tried at home, according to their own laws. To adjudicate actions of a Sicilian with a Sicilian not of the same citizenship, the praetor should appoint a judge by lot, in accordance with the decree of Publius Rupilius, which he fixed on the recommendation of the ten legates (sent to advise him at the formal organization of the province), which decree the Sicilians call the Rupilian Law. To adjudicate suits brought by an individual against a community, or by a community against an individual, the senate of another *civitas* should be assigned, granting the possibility that a *civitas* might be rejected by each side. When a Roman citizen sues a Sicilian, a Sicilian is assigned to adjudicate; when a Sicilian sues a Roman citizen, a Roman citizen is assigned. In all other matters judges are accustomed to be selected from among the Roman citizens resident in the assize district.

In Cicero's account, the legal landscape of Roman Sicily is tessellated into jurisdictions, in each of which a different system of civil law is understood to obtain.[4] Those jurisdictions are termed *civitates*, and these are understood in their totality as embracing all lands and peoples – and thus all justiciable actions – of the province. Implicit, too, in Cicero's vocabulary is the claim that systems of norms are generated by, and effective over, particularized political communities, whose membership, however determined, is juridically defined. We can grasp something of the tight connection drawn in Roman thought between the ontology of political communities and their adherence to locally generated norms in the definition provided by the textbook of law of the second-century jurist Gaius:

> Omnes populi qui legibus et moribus reguntur partim suo proprio, partim communi omnium hominum iure utuntur: nam quod quisque populus ipse sibi ius constituit, id ipsius proprium est vocaturque ius civile, quasi ius proprium civitatis; quod vero naturalis ratio inter omnes homines constituit, id apud omnes populos peraeque custoditur vocaturque ius gentium, quasi quo iure omnes gentes utuntur. populus itaque Romanus partim suo proprio, partim communi omnium hominum iure utitur. (Gaius *Institutes* 1.1)

> All peoples who are governed by statutes and customs observe partly their own peculiar law and partly the common law of all human beings. The law that a people establishes for itself is peculiar to it, and is called *ius civile*, being, as it were, the special law of that *civitas*, that community of citizens, while the law that natural reason establishes among all human beings is followed by all peoples alike, and is called *ius gentium*, being, as it were, the law observed by all peoples. Thus the Roman people observes partly its own peculiar law and partly the common law of humankind.

Again, I will discuss the essential connection in Roman thought between consent to law and political belonging in chapter 2, and I will return to this passage as part of a general consideration of Roman thinking in regard to the ontology of the social in chapter 3. For now, let me simply underline through restatement the claim here advanced, that the legitimacy and efficacy of legal systems rests upon the design and functioning of the legislative institutions that produce them: local social orders are best secured by norms generated within and by the society they are called upon to regulate.[5]

The third way of discussing jurisdiction common in classical Roman texts does so in terms of the catchments of territory and population subject to any given code of law, and the situating or siting of legal institutions within particular landscapes and built environments.[6] In this case the evidence consists in patterns of metonymy widespread in both normative and descriptive political and geographic texts, when these describe the distribution of populations across provincial landscapes; the encompassing of those populations by systems of law; and the geographic and institutional loci of systems of dispute resolution within those landscapes. Consider, for example, the account in Pliny the Elder's geographic books of a people called the Vocontii, who dwelled in Gallia Narbonensis:

Vocontiorum civitatis foederatae duo capita Vasio et Lucus Augusti.

The two capitals of Vocontii, an allied political community, namely, Vasio and Grove of Augustus. (Pliny *Nat.* 3.37)

Here, the term *civitas* refers to the totality of the political community, which is distributed across the landscape in two chief cities called *capita*, "heads," and an unspecified number of further settlements of whatever size and status. Another such example is Cemenilo, the *oppidum*, the town, of the *civitas Vediantiorum* in Liguria, the town of the political community of the Vediantii (Pliny *Nat.* 3.47). Such instances draw attention to the primacy of "community of citizens" among the meanings of *civitas* and thereby highlight the status of "city" as metonym.

To denominate a population a *civitas* was also to invoke assumptions about the juridical articulation of its population and its degree of institutional development. Thus Pliny contrasts *civitates* with *nationes* (perhaps best rendered "tribes"), the former being legally articulated political communities, the latter mere agglomerations of people united (presumably) by descent. That said, in keeping with the argument above, the decision on the part of some Roman regarding how to classify any given population into one or the other such category was to a point distinct from the question of how robust and well-furnished a nucleated settlement that population inhabited. For example, in the fifth book of the *Natural History*, Pliny surveys the 526 "peoples" (*populi*) who obey the *imperium Romanum* from the river Ambsaga to the border of Africa: these include six colonies, a number of *oppida civium Romanorum*, one *oppidum Latinum*, an *oppidum stipendiarium*, 30 *oppida libera* ... at which point Pliny gives up: *ex reliquo numero*, of the remaining number, most can rightly be called *non civitates sed nationes*.[7] Similarly, when Pliny enumerates the peoples of the Alps, he includes among them an unspecified and undifferentiated number of *Cottianae civitates*: whatever status Pliny granted their political development in deploying that term, it is unlikely that he thought their populations (*civitas*-as-*populus*) were in fact distributed across the landscape exclusively in towns, one per populace (*civitas*-as-*urbs*).[8]

The contrast between *oppidum*, town, and *civitas*, political community, then motivates the elaboration of a further apparatus with which to explain the function of nucleated settlements within the territories of such communities.[9] Consider, for example, the following descriptions of social and legal relations among populations understood as non-urbanized, dwelling in the hinterlands of Roman (urban) administrative centres:

Cicero *Verr.* 2.2.38: *Adversarii postulant ut in eam rem iudices dentur, ex iis civitatibus quae in id forum convenirent electi, qui Verri viderentur.*	The adversaries demand that *iudices* be appointed in this matter, selected from those communities of citizens who gather in the same *forum*, whoever should seem appropriate to Verres.
Pliny *Nat.* 3.26: *In Cluniensem conventum Varduli ducunt populous xiv...*	The Varduli lead 14 tribes to the assize Cluniensis ...
Pliny *Nat.* 3.26: *In eundem conventum Carietes et Vennenses v civitatibus vadunt...*	The Carietes and Vennenses go to the same assize, with five communities ...

Pliny *Nat.* 3.142: *petunt in eam (coloniam) iura viribus discriptis in decurias cccxlii Delmataei...*	The Delmataei, whose men are divided into 342 groups, seek laws in that colony ...
Pliny *Nat.* 5.109: *longinquiores eodem foro disceptant Orthronienses, Alidienses...*	Among the people further away who settle their disputes in the same forum are the Orthronienses, the Alidienses ...

In these texts, *conventus* and equally *convenire* – literally, "a coming-together" and "to come together" – are metonymic of the purpose for which people come together, namely, the holding of a judicial assize. Similarly, the naming of a Roman-style monumentalized urban core, a *forum*, can stand – by virtue of the assumption that all properly ordered cities will have one – for the functioning of depersonalized, communal institutions of dispute resolution and rights redemption, which are understood to have such a *forum* as their necessary context. In this way, *forum* suffices to identify the function of Roman-style conurbations as nodal points for the intrusion of Roman institutions into landscapes of peoples not articulated along Roman lines.

This is not to say that Pliny does not use *civitas* to refer to cities. But his usage illustrates the metonymic relationship between the notion of the political community in its most essential sense, namely, a population or community of citizens, and the urban form in which such populations achieved some telos of the human condition as conceived in ancient political and ethical philosophy, namely, the city. It follows that the use of *civitas* at any given moment to indicate any one of its meanings in some primary fashion necessarily activated the others: to speak of citizenship was thus to invoke and advance to varying degrees a further set of claims about the juridical basis of political communities, the situation of those communities within monumentalized urban cores, and the dependence of some rural catchment on those urban cores for the provision of depersonalized institutions of dispute resolution.

The use of *civitas* to refer to both political communities and their extension through space is important for numerous reasons, of which two are directly relevant to the argument of this chapter.

First, administrative and juridical mappings such as those provided by Pliny and Gaius effectively tessellate the empire *civitas* by *civitas*, within each of which a different system of law potentially obtains. Such mappings harmonize closely to modern understandings of ancient empire as a political form:[10] in these, empires are depicted as governing through the cultivation and management of difference (or perhaps I should say, "finite and tolerable difference"); constituent populations are rived, one from another, while each is interpellated as a distinct subject of imperial rule through purely bilateral relations with the metropole. Nation states, by contrast, imagine their institutions, infrastructure, and culture permeating uniformly through their territory.

But imperial mappings, which imagine *cives* dwelling in distinct *civitates*, as well as the practices of recognition and toleration that such mappings sustain, exist in fundamental tension with a variety of historical processes – some intentional, explicit, and purposive at the level of the imperial state, others accidental – that were alike inevitable consequences of empire. Among the former, one thinks in particular of grants of citizenship to elites within notionally alien communities; and among the latter, of human mobility among subaltern populations. The long-term effect of all such processes was the creation of communities whose populations were juridically heterogeneous, even as the communities themselves retained a specific and unitary legal status as a matter of public law.[11] In sum, the link between citizenship, law, community, and territoriality that was essential to Roman conceptions of empire as form, was steadily and everywhere eroded by the practice of empire in historical and demographic reality.

In the Roman case, this tension between the historical effects of empire and the presuppositions regarding territoriality that inhered in the concept of *civitas* was formally resolved by administrative fiat, namely the edict of the emperor Caracalla in 212 CE that granted Roman citizenship to nearly all freeborn residents of the empire. But another problem was thereby created, because the cognitive association of population, territory, law, and city that the term *civitas* had theretofore necessarily evoked henceforth failed. We thus witness, over the century and a half that followed Caracalla's edict, a gradual disarticulation of the concept of *civitas*-as-citizenship from that of *civitas*-as-city, such that the one could be invoked without (strongly) activating the latter, which paved the way for new movements in political theory at the gloaming of empire in the west.[12] Consider, for example, the remarkable letter from 371 CE of the emperors Valentinian, Valens, and Gratian to the proconsular governor of Asia, Eutropius, which directed revenues from imperial estates to be used for the material support of cities (the history of the scheme involves complexities that are not relevant here):[13]

> Inasmuch as we have allowed, in very truth, various *civitates* to reap a rich reward from our Liberality by assigning to each several city (*ad singulas urbes*) for the repair of its urban fabric a set portion of the estimated yield ... from the revenues of the private imperial estates in Asia: you report that by means of this new support they are rising from the unsightly desolation of recent ruins to their ancient aspect, as befits the felicity of our times. (HD021695 ll. 2–5; translation ARS)

Latent in this text's shifting usage is a potential slippage between some conception of *civitates* as autonomous political communities, with their own determinate form of self-flourishing, and *urbes*, mere agglomerations of buildings, no more and no less than aggregations of persons and material infrastructure, which exist merely in contribution to some imperial whole.

The second reason that I devote such attention to the use of *civitas* to denote populations extending through space is that this usage existed in close analogical or symbiotic relation with other apparatus for conceiving political belonging in its territorial and material dimensions. In what follows, I focus first on territoriality as conceived through borders; second on territory figured as a piece of land or, more directly, as a plot of soil; and third on a subsidiary problem of territoriality, namely contiguity.

2. Perhaps the body of law most invested in the language of borders is that concerning *postliminium*, the right of persons captured in war to recover their full legal rights, including citizenship and property rights, upon their return to Roman territory.[14] (The recovery was necessary because persons captured in war were treated in law as if dead.) In the pithy formulation of the Severan jurist Paul, "when a person returns *in fines suos*, into his

own borders, he recovers his former rights." Elsewhere Paul speaks of someone returning *in fines nostros*, "into our borders."[15] But this language is already visible in the works of the Augustan jurist Antistius Labeo, where it is employed to identify just that moment when the recovery of rights occurs:

Si id, quod nostrum hostes ceperunt, eius generis est, ut postliminio redire possit: simul atque ad nos redeundi causa profugit ab hostibus et intra fines imperii nostri esse coepit, postliminio redisse existimandum est. (Labeo *Πιθανῶν a Paulo epitomatorum* bk. 8 fr. 226 Lenel = *Dig.* 49.15.30)

If a thing of ours which the enemy captures is of such a kind that it can return by *postliminium*, then as soon as it has escaped from the enemy for the purpose of returning *ad nos*, to us, and has begun to be *intra fines imperii nostri*, within the boundaries of our empire, it is to be reckoned as having returned by *postliminium*.

Similarly, in the Carolingian abbreviation by Paul the deacon of the second-century dictionary of Festus, it is written that "he is said to have received *postliminium* who, having been captured *extra limina*, beyond the thresholds" – which term he glosses as *terminos provinciae*, "the borders of a province" – "returns *ad propria*, to his own."[16]

The term "province" draws our attention to a persistent tension in the law of *postliminium*, namely, that the legal doctrine clearly rests upon a presumption that the borders of political communities will map the territory they control, which will also define the extension of both their people and their institutions in space. But Rome was an imperial state, and many parties legally alien in respect to the metropole were subject to its rule, and it made no sense to imagine Romans losing citizenship when they left Roman territory *stricto sensu* and entered the borders of a subordinate allied king. It was reflection on just this situation that generated the famous remarks of the Julio-Claudian jurist Proculus on the operation of relations of *maiestas*, "greaterness," the antecedent of modern "majesty," in Roman foreign relations. As he remarked, there can be no relation of *postliminium* between us and free or allied peoples, "for they retain their freedom and property rights when *apud nos*, among us, as we do when *apud eos*, among them":

Liber autem populus est is, qui nullius alterius populi potestati est subiectus: sive is foederatus est item, sive aequo foedere in amicitiam venit sive foedere comprehensum est, ut is populus alterius populi maiestatem comiter conservaret. hoc enim adicitur, ut intellegatur alterum populum superiorem esse, non ut intellegatur alterum non esse liberum: et quemadmodum clientes nostros intellegimus liberos esse, etiamsi neque auctoritate neque dignitate neque viri boni nobis praesunt, sic eos, qui maiestatem nostram comiter conservare debent, liberos esse intellegendum est. (Proculus *Epistulae* bk. 8 fr. 30 Lenel = *Dig.* 49.15.7.1)

A free people is one that is not subject to the power of another people. An allied people is either one that has entered into friendship under an equal treaty or one embraced by a treaty such that one people should with good will respect the greaterness of the other. Note moreover that the one people is understood to be superior; the other is not to be understood as not free. So, just as we understand our clients to be free, even if they do not excel us in authority or dignity, so those who are bound to respect our *maiestas* with good will should be understood to be free.

We witness in these remarks a structural tension, a disconnect, even, between the presuppositions regarding territoriality inherent in the law of citizenship and doctrines of jurisdiction, on the one hand, and the presuppositions regarding territoriality inherent in Roman legal and diplomatic practice and still-born doctrines of sovereignty, on the other.

As it happens, just this concern over the non-correspondence between the mappings of the world generated by conceptual frameworks of *imperium*-as-domestic power of command, *imperium*-as-interstate hegemony, and *civitas*-as-self-governing polity is visible already in the first jurisprudential text on *postliminium* to survive, a fragment of the first-century BCE legal lexicographer Aelius Gallus, quoted in the dictionary of Festus:[17]

Postliminium receptum, Gallus Aelius in libro primo significationum, quae ad ius pertinent, ait esse eum, qui liber, ex qua civitate in aliam civitatem abierat, in eandem civitatem redit eo iure, quod constitutum est de postliminis: item qui servos a nobis in hostium potestatem pervenit, postea ad nos redit in eius potestatem, cuius antea fuit, iure postlimini. Equi et muli et navis eadem ratio est postliminium receptionis quae servi. Quae genera rerum ab hostibus ad nos postliminium redeunt, eadem genera rerum <a> nobis ad hostis redire possunt. Cum populis liberis et confoederatis et cum regibus postliminium nobis est ita, uti cum hostibus. quae nationes in dicione nostra sunt, cum his [postliminium non est]. (Festus s.v. *postliminium receptum* 244L = Aelius Gallus fr. 1 Huschke-Seckel-Kübler)

Aelius Gallus in his first book of definitions that relate to law says that he who as a free person went from some *civitas* into another *civitas* returns to the same *civitas* under the right that is established concerning *postliminium*: similarly, he who as a slave passes from us into the power of an enemy afterwards returns to us in the power of him in whose power he was before, according to the right of *postliminium*. With free peoples and allied peoples and with kings there is *postliminium* for us in the same way as with enemies. Those nations in our power, with them [there is no *postliminium*].

Set aside, if you please, the problem that Gallus and Proculus do not agree on the applicability of *postliminium* to persons travelling under whatever circumstances into the territory of free and allied peoples. I draw your attention rather to his use of *civitas*, in which the meanings "citizenship," "community," and "state" or "territory" seem to me all equally active, tightly and necessarily interanimated at each occurence. The apparent success of those classical interanimations was nonetheless already under assault from the existence of *nationes in dicione nostra*, nations in our power, whose land was alien in respect to Rome – and whose people were autonomous – but whose territory was not meaningfully foreign.

3. There existed in Roman political and legal discourse a second way to talk about belonging, jurisdiction, and territoriality, which centred on soil, *solum*. It was of course capable of providing substantively identical statements of doctrine as the language of borders. It must also have formally mapped the same space as public-law concepts such *ager publicus*, whose meaning in the

classical period ranged from something like "Roman territory" to the more precise "agricultural land belonging collectively to the Roman people." But the network of associations mobilized by the notion of "soil" was quite other than that interanimated by talk of borders and was, I think, even more capacious than that mobilized by agricultural land.

One might begin by observing the capacity of soil, as opposed to borders, to motivate, or provide a locus for, affective attachment. For example, speaking before an assembly of the people, Cicero observes in his fourth invective against Catiline that, "The whole body of freeborn (citizens) is here. There is not one of us for whom the temples, the sight of the *urbs*, the possession of liberty, the very light itself and *solum patriae*, the soil of our fatherland, are not dear and delightful...."[18] Likewise, in his fifth book, Livy represents Camillus ordering his men to fight the Gauls for possession of Rome, having in their sight "the temples of the gods, their wives and children, and *solum patriae*, the soil of our fatherland, scarred by the evils of war."[19] Livy writes in similar terms in the preface to book 2 when he observes that it had been good for Rome to be ruled at first by kings, to allow the tokens of wives and children and *caritas ipsius soli*, love of the soil itself, to bind their spirits, each to the others."[20] (I will take up the temporality and contingency of that process in chapter 2.)

The capacity of "soil" to receive and nurture affection arose, I suggest, from its materiality. Unsurprisingly, a related metaphorical complex treated the soil as the stuff on which one was born or as itself generative. Earlier in Livy's fifth book, the same Camillus had opposed a motion to move the people of Rome to a new city. He urged the senators to speak out, to fight on behalf of altars, hearths, the temples of the gods – and *solo in quo nati essent*, "the soil on which they had been born."[21] Later in Livy, another general excites the soldiery against Hannibal by describing the Carthaginians as seeking to drive the Romans *solo patrio terraque in qua geneti forent*, "from their ancestral soil and the land on which they had been born."[22] Such sentiments are expressed in compressed form in later Augustan literature using phrases like *natale solum* and *solum genitale*, language expanded by Livy to make the maternal metaphor explicit: "Does the *solum patriae* have so little grip on us, nor this land that we call mother?"[23]

But though talk of soil, land, and earth often leads to such biological language and interanimates discourses of maternity, it does not inevitably lead to such. What counts, at times, is mere materiality, that soil, itself, is the stuff of *patria*. Consider, for example, Pliny the Elder's account of the power of Vestal Virgins to capture runaway slaves, part of a larger consideration of the power of prayer:

Vestales nostras hodie credimus nondum egressa urbe mancipia fugitiva retinere in loco precatione, cum, si semel recipiatur ea ratio et deos preces aliquas exaudire aut ulllis moveri verbis, confitendum sit de tota coniectatione. (Pliny *Nat.* 28.13)

We believe today that our Vestals *retinere in loco*, root to the spot, runaway slaves by means of prayer, provided they have not left the city, and yet, if this view is once admitted, that the gods hear certain prayers or are moved by any words whatsoever, the whole question must be answered in the affirmative.

The belief to which Pliny refers is naturally connected to legal–religious concepts regarding the sacrality of place, in which notions of boundary are naturally implicated. Much scholarly labour has been devoted to these. But the importance of materiality to place has been relatively neglected. Consider again the diction of Livy's Camillus:

Vrbem auspicato inauguratoque conditam habemus; nullus locus in ea non religionum deorumque est plenus. (Livy 5.52.2)

"We have a city, an *urbs*, founded by auspices and duly inaugurated; no place in it is not filled by religious scruple and by gods."

The language of fullness here responds to its usage earlier in the book, when the city had by contrast been *hostium plena*, full of enemies.[24] The city is thus not simply a two-dimensional space demarcated on a plane; it has volume and can be filled and must be touched.

It is in any event in material objects – in soil – that efficacious religious action takes hold and abides. I have elsewhere explored the synecdochic relationship of *sagmina*, the clumps of grass with their roots and soil intact used in religious and legal ritual, to the stuff of Rome itself: Roman priests, we are told, carried such clumps abroad in order to swear oaths over treaties while in contact with Roman soil, which relationship I cite here not only by way of reminding us not to forget the material and gestural correlates to the linguistic practices at issue in this study, but also to urge that we pay attention to the commitments to those aspects of social life that are visible *in* language.[25] Within a history of language, we might turn first to Varro's recollection of the types of land subject to religious law and so susceptible to particular religious actions. In that system, the principal taxon is *ager*, field or territory: "According to our state augurs, there are five types of *ager*."[26] Institutionally one might define these through the drawing of boundaries, but boundaries are the means by which space and place are defined; they are not of them. Hence the focus on territory and place, *ager* and *locus*, in the siting of camps and conduct of augural rites. To cite Varro again, from his *Calenus*: "when about to enter enemy territory, out of religious scruple generals would first throw a spear into that territory, in order to seize a place for a camp."[27] The language of territory and place matters for metaphysical reasons, because of their materiality, because they consist of soil. As the consul Valerius Corvus reminded soldiers regarding an encampment, you have your camp "*non ... in Samnio nec in Volscis sed in Romano solo*, not in Samnium nor among the Voscians, but on Roman soil."[28] It matters that Roman soldiers sleep on Roman soil.

The importance of soil as material receptor of religious action is all the more visible in the famous correspondence between Pliny and Trajan regarding the scruple involved when moving a temple. Pliny as governor of Bithynia-Pontus consulted the emperor regarding a request by the city of Nicomedia to move its temple of the Mother of the Gods. Pliny hesitated to approve the act because the temple had no *lex*, no law or regulation, as "the method of consecration" practised in Nicomedia was *alium apud nos*, "different from that practised among us." Trajan responded that Pliny could be "without fear of violating religious scruple," because the *solum peregrinae civitatis capax non sit dedicationis, quae fit nostro iure*, "as the soil of an alien *civitas* is not capacious of consecration as it is performed according to our law."[29]

We have already seen how the metonymic reach of *civitas* shifted, as the realities created by imperial political and juridical action raced ahead of linguistic–cognitive apparatus and assumptions of homeomorphy between the geographic extension of political communities and territorial reach of their jurisdictions began to break down. A similar tension is already visible in respect to religious law in remarks of Gaius on the status of provincial soil, in which every articulation of a strict principle is immediately undermined by the realities of practice and scruple in an imperial state:[30]

Sed sacrum quidem hoc solum existimatur, quod ex auctoritate populi Romani consecratum est, veluti lege de ea re lata aut senatusconsulto facto. Religiosum vero nostra voluntate facimus mortuum inferentes in locum nostrum ... Sed in provinciali solo placet plerisque solum religiosum non fieri, quia in eo solo dominium populi Romani est vel Caesaris, nos autem possessionem tantum vel usumfructum habere videmur; utique tamen, etiamsi non sit religiosum, pro religioso habetur. Item quod in provinciis non ex auctoritate populi Romani consecratum est, proprie sacrum non est, tamen pro sacro habetur. (Gaius *Inst.* 2.5–7)

That alone is thought to be sacred, which is consecrated on the authority of the Roman people, either by law or by decree of the Senate. We make things "religious" through decisions of our own[31] by bearing our dead to particular sites.... But *in provinciali solo*, on provincial soil it is generally agreed that the soil cannot be "religious," since there ownership rests with the Roman people or with Caesar, while we seem to have only possession or use. Nevertheless, even if it is not *religiosum*, it is treated as though it were. Similarly, whatever in the provinces is not consecrated on authority of the Roman people is properly not sacred, but it is nevertheless treated *pro sacro*, as if it were.

I will devote some time in the next chapter to the relationship between substitution, analogy, and fiction in classical law. In the present context I draw your attention to three things only: the elevation of soil over territory to a status of legal primary; the importance of soil as recipient of ritual action; and the simultaneous sustaining and upending of a legal principle inherent in the use of fiction: the absolute distinction between Roman and alien soil is nominally honoured, even as the substitive *pro* potentially assimilates the whole of the latter to the status of the former in practice.

Trajan's use of *civitas* returns us from the problematics of soil and religious law to those of soil and citizenship, and hence to the territorial and material aspects of political belonging. The two concepts receive conjoined articulation above all in the language of exile. Here it is crucial to remember that under the Republic, at least, exile was not a punishment. Rather, it was conceived as a process of voluntary denaturalization, by which one escaped certain punishments by removing oneself from Roman jurisdiction.[32] This removal was effected above all through geographic displacement: the idiom was *vertere* (occasionally *mutare*) *solum*, "to change soil."[33] Furthermore, authors under the Republic consistently maintained that denaturalization could only occur with the consent of the individual concerned.[34]

The deep interdependence between these conceptual domains, which is to say, between territoriality, materiality, and political belonging, emerges with particular clarity through examination of the discursive apparatus employed by Cicero and Livy to discuss exile. Livy generally employs a shorthand: *solum vertere exsilii causa*, "to change soil for the sake of exile."[35] But it is clear from the narratives that attend such usage that he understands exile to involve a change in citizenship, for which the change of soil stands in a relation of cognitive homology. So, for example, when Quinctius Caeso went into exile, "he departed *in Tuscos in exsilium*, into/among the Etruscans, into exile."[36] Likewise, when the the family of the last king, the Tarquins, were persuaded to leave Rome at the foundation of the Republic, the removal of Lucius Tarquinius to Lavinium is described using the phrase, *civitate cessit*, a removal at once from the state and membership in the state.[37] Finally, when Camillus, the hero of book 5, was in exile at Ardea, he is described as addressing the Ardeates as follows: *veteres amici, novi etiam cives mei*, "Old friends, and now my new fellow citizens." The change in place and soil entailed a change in citizenship, and vice versa.[38]

Not surprisingly, these issues receive more extended reflection in Cicero. He considers them under two rubrics, loss and change of citizenship, *mutatio civitatis*. So, for example, in his oration *pro Quinctio* he argues that it was a violation of a citizen's rights that the property of his client Quinctius had been seized, for "he is not said to have changed soil for the sake of exile" (*neque exsilii causa solum vertisse diceretur*).[39] In other words, because he did not change soil, he remains a citizen and retains his rights. Similarly, in a famous passage in the *pro Caecina*, he elaborates on the problematics of denaturalization, exile, and change of soil in the following way: Exile is not a punishment. When people want to *avoid* punishment, *eo solum vertunt, hoc est, sedem ac locum mutant*, "for this reason they change soil, which is to say, they exchange seat and place." If they consent to remain *in civitate*, then they must needs suffer the force of the law and would lose their citizenship only with their life.[40] Otherwise, one loses citizenship when one is received *in exsilium, hoc est, in aliam civitatem*, "one is received into exile, which is to say, into another *civitas*." Here again, *civitas* must refer to a polity and a place.[41]

The tight interconnection between these discursive, legal, and metaphorical apparatus is revealed by an explanatory move made by Cicero in a related passage in *De domo sua*, where again he reflects on the inability of states to deprive citizens of citizenship against their will:

> Qui cives Romani in colonias Latinas proficiscebantur fieri non poterant Latini, nisi erant auctores facti nomenque dederant: qui erant rerum capitalium condemnati non prius hanc civitatem amittebant quam erant in eam recepti, quo vertendi, hoc est mutandi, soli causa venerant. (Cicero *De domo sua* 78)

> Those Roman citizens who set out into Latin colonies could not have become Latins unless they were authors of the deed and handed in their names. Those who have been condemned on capital charges did not lose this *civitas* until they had been received into the one where they had come for the sake of changing, which is to say, exchanging their soil.

Here, Cicero performs one reversal and gives one explanation. He reverses the language of Livy, who tends to gloss "change soil" with "for the sake of exile," in which phraseology the change of citizenship is implicit in the idiom and the action. In Cicero, by contrast, the primary action is explicitly the change of citizenship – that being the subject of the passage, rather than exile, which is but one circumstance under which such changes take place. When I say that Cicero gives an explanation, I mean that he glosses *vertere*, the idiomatic verb for a change of soil, with *mutare*, the common verb for a change of citizenship. To gloss *vertere solum* with *mutare solum* is to bring the idiomatic (metaphor) and the legal (metaphor) into explicit synonymity.

The potential that inheres in these complexes, to conceive *civitates* as extending through space and resting on matter, finds further expression in somewhat rarer metaphorical complexes where a change of citizenship is figured as a journey. Consider, for example, Cicero's remarks on change of citizenship in the speech *pro Balbo*:

Iure enim nostro neque mutare civitatem quisquam invitus potest, neque si velit mutare non potest, modo adsciscatur ab ea civitate cuius esse se civitatis velit ... <cum> hanc ante amittere non potuissent quam hoc solum civitatis mutatione vertissent, sed etiam postliminio potest civitatis fieri mutatio. (Cicero *Balb.* 27)

Under our law, no one can be made to exchange citizenship if unwilling, nor, if willing, can anyone be prevented from doing so, so long as he is taken up by that *civitas*, of whose *civitas* he wishes to be. [Having named various individuals who declared themselves to other states for the sake of exile, he continues:] since they could not have lost this *civitas* before they had changed this soil by means of an exchange of *civitas*; *mutatio civitatis*, exchange of citizenship can also occur by means of *postliminium*.

Quod si civi Romano licet esse Gaditanum sive exsilio sive postliminio sive reiectione huius civitatis ... quid est quam ob rem civi Gaditano in hanc civitatem venire non liceat? Equidem longe secus sentio. Nam cum ex omnibus civitatibus via sit in nostram, cumque nostris civibus pateat ad ceteras iter civitates ... (Cicero *Balb.* 29)

But if a Roman citizen might become a Gaditanus (a citizen of Gades) through exile or *postliminium* or surrender of this citizenship... on what grounds can a citizen of Gades not come *in hanc civitatem*, into this *civitas*? I can't think of any. For since from every *civitas* there exists a path into this one, and since for our citizens *pateat ad ceteras iter civitates*, a going – a route or journey – lies open to other *civitates* …

So, Cicero concludes, the more closely communities are tied to Rome, the more open the two citizenships should be to members of the two communities. As regards the themes of this chapter, please observe how the usage of *via* and *iter*, path and route or journey, reflects by inversion the relation of *civitas*-qua-citizenship to *civitas*-qua-territory-embodied-as-soil. With *civitas*, it is tempting to identify the abstraction "citizenship" as the primary meaning, of which "state" is metonym by way of some cognitive commitment to the materiality of territoriality. In the case of paths and routes, the materiality of practice might be regarded as primary, from which some meaning like "means" or "way" is ideated. But Cicero's language – as well as the direction of his explanatory gestures – suggests rather a momentary inextricability of their imbrication: changes *of civitas* were always moves *into civitates*, as Cicero's own prepositions confirm.

Let me close by gesturing at one final domain of inquiry, that of contiguity. What was at stake in Roman conceptions of belonging, in the figuring of belonging as attachment to soil? Was soil merely a signifier in some discourse about territoriality, which was itself nothing more (and nothing less) than a principle of adjudication, a rule for distinguishing citizen and alien? Just over a decade ago, I published an essay in which I traced a preliminary history of arguments from ecological determinism in Roman politics and literature.[42] This is the theory that the ecology of a site contributes to, even overdetermines, the character of persons who live there. Can we find some such principle underlying Roman commitments to materiality as a component of political belonging, as these are instantiated in the discourse of soil?

A full exploration of this topic is not possible here, but let me gesture at two areas of inquiry, both arising from what I call contiguity. Was there any feeling that Romans should live not simply on land legally Roman, but that the extension of the Roman people and Roman territory through space should be continuous, that they should be bound both to one another and to Rome by some material means, that land legally Roman should touch other land legally Roman until, like all roads, all land would lead one back to Rome?

One response lies buried in a missing portion of Livy, in the history of Roman tribes.[43] Until the final third of the third century BCE, significant additions to Roman territory were incorporated into the public-law structures of the state through the creation of new "tribes." These were units of citizens, employed to sort voters, like parliamentary ridings or contributions to the American electoral college, but they were defined in space. One acquired a tribal identity by residence within a tribe's territory: citizens changed tribe when they moved. At some point between 232 BCE and the start of Livy's twenty-first book in 218 – perhaps in the context of the census of the year 220 covered in Livy book 20 – the decision was made *not* to add new tribes to embrace the territory north of the Apennines annexed through an agrarian law passed a decade earlier. Instead, new communities were simply assigned to pre-existing tribes that were located south of the Apennines. The geographic – the material – contiguity that bound members of tribes to one another was at this moment forever fractured.[44] A new wrinkle was added in the early imperial period (if not before) when, in a series of cases, emperors settled colonies of veterans inside pre-existing communities and assigned the new residents to tribes other than the one to which the community had previously belonged. In this moment, the geographic and material specificity of the tribal system would seem to have been altogether deracinated, tribal identity now being abstracted as a marker of identity that interpellated an individual in respect to the state in a purely transcendental manner.[45]

A second (related) area of practice and discourse wherein one might investigate the principles that attend or undergird this commitment to materiality, whether in the form of contiguity or otherwise, is colonialism. It would be difficult to overstate the areas of difference between Greek and Roman practice, law, and ideology in respect to colonization. Most pressing in this context is the Roman insistence that colonies were not in any way autonomous communities but rather were substituent parts of the Roman state. The Romans therefore had no linguistic apparatus that could capture the distinction between a city and its colony, and the potential for rivalry between them, that remained an essential correlate to the language of kinship in Greek colonialist diplomacy. The word "metropolis," for example, enters Latin through transliteration in civic inscriptions of Asia Minor only at the turning of the second to the third century CE.[46] What would the word say in Latin? Maternity expresses a relation between two entities with distinct and equivalent ontologies: it was therefore wholly unsuitable to Roman colonialism.

When the Romans did refer to Greek colonialism, they therefore employed their own terms of art: "Among the most harmful of the laws of Gracchus," writes Velleius Paterculus, "is that he placed colonies outside Italy."

> This our ancestors avoided, when they saw how much more powerful Carthage was than Tyre, Massilia than Phocaea, Syracuse than Corinth, Cyzicus and Byzantium than Miletus, their *genitali solo*, their generative soil, and they summoned Roman citizens from the provinces back to Italy to be censused. (Velleius 2.7.7)

Please observe that Velleius implicitly construes Italy as uniform, Roman citizens being summoned there as to a single and selfsame soil. The problem of the non-contiguity of Roman territory within Italy – or, one might say, of Italy's internal ecological heterogeneity – is not visible to Velleius because he wrote more than a century after the integration of Italy in both citizenship and law. As theories of ecological determinism had once helped to explain the political heterogeneity of Italy by reference to the natural, to wit, its ecological diversity, so, in the aftermath of its political unification, such background understandings demanded a recalibration of Italian nature. In the lifetime of Cicero, by contrast, it had still been possible to object that the placement of colonies in Campania, scant miles from Rome, would be dangerous because the climate would engender arrogance.[47] When but a single generation had passed since the unification of Italy through civil war, it remained possible to conceive it as ecologically and therefore politically heterogeneous. By Velleius's day, summoning citizens "back to Italy" was effectively the same as bringing them "back to Rome": the universality of Roman citizenship within Italy now being taken for granted, understandings of Italy as an ecology and its relationship to Rome as political centre had both changed.

That said, for all its theoretical interest, the history of these pre-articulate commitments may now be lost to us, the texts that survive having largely been written long after such commitments could be meaningfully sustained. Nonetheless, I close by citing two instantiations only of the long-lived nature of these apparatus. Over the course of the fifth century, the Romans gradually ceded territories in Gaul and along the Danube to foreign control. That control was construed by Salvian as consisting above all in being subjugated to a barbarian system of law, and his own condition was materially that of an alien or exile, living *in alieno solo*, on foreign soil.[48] In the same period Eugippius describes Saint Severinus of Noricum admonishing civilians in the face of barbarian onslaught to migrate *in Romani soli provinciam*, "to a province of Roman soil."[49]

As a matter of law, neither Gallic nor Norican soil had ever been "Roman." But when Salvian and Eugippius sought language with which to claim a Romanness that was even then vanishing in historical reality, the language available for staking such a claim was a metaphorical apparatus that tied person to soil to citizenship. Even at the twilight of empire, the niceties of law yielded to the materiality of belonging and the abiding power of metaphor.

CHAPTER TWO

Cognition

Tropes are [expressions] that distort a word from its proper and native signification to an improper and alien one... There seem to be two causes for such changes, necessity and ornament. By necessity, thus: Since words are the signs of things, as the jurisconsult says, and there are many more things in nature than words, and since every language lacks its own word for many things, in such cases other words must be summoned.

– Giambattista Vico[1]

1. The topic of this second chapter might be described in two ways. On the one hand, it seeks to survey essential structures of Latinate Roman cognition, by which I intend linguistic instantiations of characteristic modes of reasoning: metaphor and metonymy; analogy and comparison; ideation and abstraction. At the same time, in order to sustain certain continuities of theme and argument with chapter 1, I concentrate here on evidence arising from normative texts concerned with law and government. Beyond the very basic ambition of placing cognition on the agenda of classical scholarship, I wish here to advance the claim that Roman government was made possible in part by a distinctive capacity on the part of classical Romans for ideation and analogical reasoning.

By "Roman government" I intend two things. First, the Roman empire was enormously variegated, at the level of ecology, economy, language, and every aspect of culture, dress, cuisine, you name it. To be governed, this world had to be described and regulated. The question was how to do this, in a fashion that gave appropriate and effective recognition to the particularity of the empire's myriad cultural systems without reproducing within the empire's systems of law and administration the chaotic diversity of the world it oversaw.[2] The second sense in which I employ the term "government" concerns the functioning of republican empire. Rome used the law of persons generally, and grants of full and deficient forms of citizenship more specifically, to grow the state and extend its power. How was the extension of citizenship – how was the making of Romans, or the taking-up of Romanness – theorized (and practised), such that the heterogeneity of the persons incorporated did not radically and essentially destabilize the self-understanding of the metropolitan centre?[3]

2. Let me start with the problem of normative language, and with a seemingly minor example, namely, acorns. In a work on the establishing of boundaries by one Hyginus, transmitted in the corpus of Roman land surveyors (the text appears to date from the late second or early third century), he reflects briefly on the ways professional practice must adapt to the discrete conditions of the various provinces:

> Our profession is not so narrowly restricted that it cannot regulate the distinctive observation of boundaries in the individual provinces. Lands yielding revenue have many different forms (*multas constitutiones*). In some provinces, [landholders] pay a definite proportion of the produce, some one-fifth, others one-seventh; others pay cash, and this is based on an evaluation of the land. Definite values have been established for lands; for example, in Pannonia there are first-class lands (*arui primi*), second-class lands (*arui secundi*), meadows (*prati*), acorn-bearing woods (*silvae glandiferae*), ordinary woods (*silvae vulgaris*), and pasture land (*pascuae*). (Hyginus *Constitutio Limitum* 160.27–162.2 Campbell; translation after Brian Campbell)

Hyginus proffers "acorn-bearing woods" as an example of the land surveyer's ability to insert regional, ecologically specific categories into a generic, non-ecologically specific taxonomy. By "non-ecologically specific," I point to descriptors like "first- and second-class," which presumably could exist anywhere, as, frankly, could "pasture." But what should we make of the choice of "acorn-bearing woods" as example, or the existence of the category in the first place? The category can scarcely have been unique to Pannonia. The northern Po Valley was surely rich in acorns; it certainly produced enormous quantities of pork. "Acorn-bearing woods" must have existed as a taxon distinct from ordinary woods because of their economic utility, and what is more, the category is likely to have existed within some overall repertoire of categories of land, ready to be inserted into regional or provincial schema.[4] Certainly on those occasions when wood inserts itself into the historical record as narrated by literary sources, the justification normally lies in its utility during some contingent human engagement with the environment: one thinks immediately of the story of Larignum/*larignum* and its simultaneous encompassing by Roman power and incorporation into Latin language.[5]

But buried in these remarks lies another puzzle, dearer to my heart. The question now on the mind of all readers, I am sure, is whether Roman land surveyors also employed categories like *iuglandiferae silvae*, walnut-bearing woods, or *balaniferae silvae*, chestnut-bearing woods, and so forth. So far as I can tell, the answer is no. Very few nuts are mentioned in the great mass of Roman legal sources, despite the prominence of nuts of many kinds in Latin scientific and agricultural writing. The fondness of the agricultural writers for the term *balanus* is not matched by any on the part of the jurists: the term appears only twice in the entirety of the Digest. What is more, a quick correlation of Pliny's books on trees against the corpus of legal texts reveals no mention in the latter of cedar, a single reference to cypress, and so forth – indeed, the jurists exhibit not the slightest echo of Pliny's enthusiasm for the sheer variety of edible acorns. This, despite the fact that land surveyors working for the Roman state seized by eminent domain and marked with boundary stones immense tracts of cedar-producing forest in Lebanon as imperial properties.[6]

The explanation for this pattern clearly does not lie in a lack of interest on the part of Roman government in economic activity. It lies, rather, in the contingent use of *glans* in an early Roman legal text – the Twelve Tables – and more crucially in the subsequent development of logical, linguistic, and cognitive resources for making the application of that term to multiple fruits in varied contexts persuasive and efficacious.

The exact wording of the clause from the Twelve Tables is, alas, lost to us, as is its placement in that code. But references to it make clear that the clause treated the right to collect acorns that fell onto the property of person A from a tree located on the property of person B. We are, alas, in no position to say whether the Twelve Tables covered the right of person A to harvest the acorns that fell from another's tree, or the right of person B to enter the property of person A to recover the acorns that fell from his tree. Whatever the Twelve Tables had said, their prescriptions were modified by a clause in the praetor's edict. It apparently laid down that the owner of the tree could gather the acorns, the *glandes*, that fell from his tree on the third day from their falling, and it forbade the owner of the land on which they fell employ force to prevent him so gathering.[7] A problem related to the one that interests me arises in respect to the terms *legere* and *colligere*, the words that I translate as "gather": it is clear from another text by Ulpian, excerpted from bk. 41 of his work *Ad Sabinum* – a book concerned with theft – that the question arose whether an action might be brought when the property owner looses his herd and it grazes on the acorns (the term is *glans*). Could grazing by a herd of cattle qualify as "gathering?" It appears that the answer was no.[8] Pomponius said that the owner of the tree could bring an action *ad exhibendum*, for delivery, if the owner of the herd had loosed it *dolo*, fraudently, namely, with an intent that it should consume the *glans*, the acorns – the point being that if the acorns had been lying on the ground, the landowner could not prevent the tree owner from entering his property every third day to gather them. Ulpian, who cites this view, agrees, and adds that one could obtain an interdict allowing such gathering, though one could be compelled to acquire insurance against damage caused while the gathering went on.[9]

If one pursued only the history of interpretation in respect to "gathering," one could easily come away with the impression that the Romans had an unhealthy obsession with acorns to the neglect of all other fruit, acorns being nearly the only thing they "gather." But this was in fact not the case, the praetor's declining to expand upon the fruits named in the Twelve Tables notwithstanding. Consider the following:

glandis appellatione omnis fructus continetur, ut Iavolenus ait, exemplo Graeci sermonis, apud quos omnes arborum species ἀκρόδρυα appellantur. (Gaius bk. 4 *ad legem duodecim tabularum* fr. 438 = *Dig.* 50.16.236.1)

All fruit is included in the term "acorn" (*glandis appellatione*), as Javolenus says, *exemplo Graeci sermonis*, on analogy with the Greek language, among whom [*sic*] all types of trees are called ἀκρόδρυα ≈ "high oaks."

Ait praetor: "glandem, quae ex illius agro in tuum cadat, quo minus illi tertio quoque die legere auferre liceat, vim fieri veto." Glandis nomine omnes fructus continentur. (Ulpian bk. 71 *ad edictum* fr. 1613 Lenel = *Dig.* 43.28.*pr.*-1)

The praetor says, "I forbid the use of force to prevent someone from gathering and taking away on the third day acorns that fall from his land into yours." *Omnes fructus*, all fruits are embraced by the word "acorn" (*glandis nomine*).

In these passages, the term "acorn" is granted status as a universal metonym for all fruit (and possibly nuts) that grow on trees. To these passages – and their method, on which more later – compare a passage from the twenty-fifth book of Ulpian's *Ad Sabinum*, which likewise considers the semantic range of terms in legal language and the interpretive principles by which these might be extended:

Ligni appellatio nomen generale est, sed sic separatur, ut sit aliquid materia, aliquid lignum. materia est, quae ad aedificandum fulciendum necessaria est, lignum, quidquid conburendi causa paratum est. sed utrum ita demum, si concisum sit an et si non sit? et Quintus Mucius libro secundo refert, si cui ligna legata essent, quae in fundo erant, arbores quidem materiae causa succisas non deberi.... Ofilius quoque libro quinto iuris partiti ita scripsit, cui ligna legata sunt, ad eum omnia ligna pertinere, quae alio nomine non appellantur, veluti virgae carbones nuclei olivarum, quibus ad nullam aliam rem nisi ad comburendum possit uti: sed et balani vel si qui alii nuclei.

Lignorum appellatione in quibusdam regionibus, ut in aegypto, ubi harundine pro ligno utuntur, et harundines et papyrum comburitur et herbulae quaedam vel spinae vel vepres continebuntur. quid mirum? cum ξύλον hoc et naves ξυληγὰς appellant, quae haec ἀπὸ τῶν ἑλῶν deducunt. In quibusdam provinciis et editu bubum ad hanc rem utuntur.

...

de pinu autem integri strobili ligni appellatione continebuntur. (Ulpian bk. 25 *Ad Sabinum* fr. 2679 Lenel = *Dig.* 32.55 & 50.16.167)

The term *lignum* is a general term but one should distinguish between *materia*, "timber," which is one thing, and *lignum*, "firewood," which is another.[10] *Materia* is that which is necessary for building and supporting; *lignum* is that which has been readied for burning. Is wood one or the other, if it has been cut up or not? In his second book Quintus Mucius says that if the *ligna* (qua "firewood") on a farm has been left as a legacy, trees cut up for timber are not owed ... Ofilius in the fifth book of his *Classification of Law* wrote: if *ligna* are left to someone as a legacy, all *ligna* belong to him that are not designated by some other name (*quae alio nomine non appellantur*), such as twigs, charcoal, and olive pits, which can be used for nothing other than burning, and also *balani* and any other nuts (*sed et balani vel si qui alii nuclei*). ...

In certain regions, for example in Egypt, where reeds are used *pro ligno*, in the place of wood, reeds and papyrus are burned, and these, as well as certain grasses and thorns and briars, are all embraced as *lignorum appellatione*, under the term "wood." Why the surprise? For they call it ξύλον, "wood," and they call the boats ξυληγὰς, "wood-hauling" that bring it ἀπὸ τῶν ἑλῶν, from the marshes. In certain provinces they even use cowdung for this purpose. ...

Whole cones from the pine are included *ligni appellatione*, under the term "firewood."

The question before the jurists, and before the praetor, and before all those who had relations with neighbours mediated by property, was how things that were not acorns could be regulated by a law that nominally concerned itself only with them – or one might say, how could the law be made to operate such that things that were not acorns could be governed by the law of acorns. In this case, the existence of a second-order generic, "fruit," permitted the subordination of all other particulars to the one, acorn, which was henceforth understood to stand synecdochically for the whole, although in any given application it would probably be more accurate to say that "acorn" stands for "peach," say, by a dependent metonymy.[11] Except that acorns are not obviously fruit, but nuts, which is to say they are one of "the other *nuclei*," to use the language of Ulpian.

Ulpian's text brings to the fore the tension between imperial heterogeneity and metropolitan language that is a structural feature of all imperial epistemes: observe, inter alia, Ulpian's use of Greek in discussing Egypt, as though marking the foreignness of the phenomenon that requires explanation by asserting that it can only be explained through recourse to pseudo-native terminology – pseudo-native because, of course, Greek was only the language of Egypt as the result of earlier imperial action. Consider, too, the means by which papyrus and other reeds are embraced within the law of *lignum*: they are emphatically not wood but are used in practice, and treated at law, *pro ligno*, as if they were. The exact nature of the cognitive and taxonomic operations conducted by the phrases *nomine* or *appellatione continetur* is thus left deeply underspecified.

The remainder of this chapter is structured around three devices we have already witnessed in operation, which I now highlight and treat in turn: analogy, fiction, and abstraction.

3. Analogical reasoning rests upon acts of comparison. It interests me because it stretches the act of comparison beyond single aspects of unitary objects to more complex acts of abstraction and intellection – beyond mere homeomorphy, as it were, to homology. That said, all comparison rests upon decisions to foreground certain axes of analysis as primary, while allowing others to recede into the background after the fashion of ceteris paribus assumptions, all against some baseline relationship of similarity sufficient to legitimate the comparison in the first place. The assertion that donuts and coffee mugs are homeomorphic, for

example, is only meaningful in light of a decision to foreground shape and neglect chemical composition, density, and colour, as well as, perhaps, ontology.

The Latin term that most often flags the operation of analogy is *exemplum*: some situation should be handled *ad exemplum legis Aquiliae, ad exemplum venditionis*, and so on.[12] In such cases, we should understand legal reasoning as occurring through generic narratives or conceptual models. When parties approach the law, the messy stuff of daily life is macerated and sorted by the machinery of legal reasoning; certain facts – a very narrow range of facts – are deemed salient; and a fit is declared between the particular concerns of select individuals in their mutual relations and the narrative or model that serves as the lens of the law upon the world. When the jurists assert that some case must be treated after the pattern of, or on analogy with, some action, they acknowledge an imperfect fit – it is the fact of non-straightforwardness that generates the need for analogy in the first place. I am particularly charmed by those moments when the jurists feel some anxiety about the aptness of the analogy, which they flag by the insertion of some word such as *quodammodo*, "somehow," as in, "A should be understood somehow on analogy with B." In some cases, the detail that differentiates the case at hand from the model being applied is flagged in analysis, or simply stated through the use of *vice/vicem* – "situation A can be understood on analogy with situation B, with X functioning in the place of Y."[13] A favourite of mine, because colourful rather than intellectually elaborate, concerns the procedure to be applied when a soldier or magistrate is accused of adultery. Normally cases of adultery had to be resolved within 60 days of the charges being made. A regular exception was made for persons in state employ who could be expected to be away from Rome on state business. Those persons as a class could not be indicted on a charge of adultery, triggering the 60-day window, as long as they were absent without intent of evasion.[14] But what about soldiers serving in the night watch of the city of Rome or the urban cohort?

Quod si quis praesens sit, vice tamen absentis habetur (ut puta qui in uigilibus vel urbanis castris militat), dicendum est deferri hunc posse:

neque enim laborare habet, ut se repraesentet. (Ulpian *[Ad legem Iuliam] de adulteriis* bk. 2 fr. 1949 Lenel = *Dig.* 48.5.16.3)

But if someone who is present is nevertheless treated in the place of the absent person [imagined by judicial norms] – as, for example, someone serving in the *vigiles* or the urban cohorts [to wit, a soldier serving in the city of Rome] – it should be stated that he can be accused, for he does not have to take any pains to put in an appearance.

To paraphrase: if a person was in fact present who would otherwise be presumed absent, he could be accused – though the status of the normative presumption would normally require that in such cases he be treated *as if* absent. The fact of actual presence is allowed, *mirabile dictu,* to trump the presumption of a legal fact of absence.

Comparisons are frequently made and analogies drawn using the vocabulary of geographic proximity or neighbourliness, especially *vicinitas* and *vicinus, -a, -um.*[15] Consider, for example, the definition of *denominatio* (metonymy) offered in the early first-century BCE handbook of rhetoric, the *Rhetorica ad Herennium*:

Denominatio est quae ab rebus propinquis et finitimis trahit orationem qua possit intelligi res quae non suo vocabulo sit appellata. (*Rhet. ad Herennium* 5.43)

Metonymy is the figure that draws *ab rebus propinquis et finitimis,* from nearby or neighbouring things, an expression by which an object not being called by its own name can be understood.

Likewise, as an abstract principle, for example, the jurist Julian urged that in those cases where there exists no applicable statute, one ought to follow the practice established by custom and usage; and where these are lacking, one should cleave to that "which is closest to and entailed by it," meaning, one supposes, that which is analogically most proximate.[16] More concretely, the Severan jurist Paul quotes the Trajanic jurist Titius Aristo as saying that since barter is *vicina emptioni,* proximate to sale, the same implicit warranties govern the exchange of slaves through barter as through sale.[17] Indeed, if one pursues the law of barter down through the ages, one is exposed to nearly the full range of Latin vocabulary in respect to analogy, and more than that.[18] For barter was emphatically *not* sale, and it was always possible to assert their difference rather than likeness, distance rather than proximity.

Et si quidem pecuniam dem, ut rem accipiam, emptio et venditio est: sin autem rem do, ut rem accipiam, quia non placet permutationem rerum emptionem esse, dubium non est nasci civilem obligationem, in qua actione id veniet, non ut reddas quod acceperis, sed ut damneris mihi, quanti interest mea illud de quo convenit accipere. (Paul bk. 5 *Quaestionum* fr. 1322 Lenel = *Dig.* 19.5.5.1)

If I give you money in order to receive something, that is *emptio et venditio*, sale and purchase. But if I give you a thing in order to receive a thing, because it is agreed that exchange of things [i.e., barter] is not sale, there is no doubt that a civil-law obligation arises, in which action the issue will not be that you return what you took, but rather that you recompense me for my interest in that which it was agreed I would receive.

Paul's comments here are cryptic because terse and incomplete: by his time, the difference between barter and sale seemed to have been thoroughly worked out – or perhaps one should say the extent and nature of areas of disagreement about that difference appeared to be settled – and reference might be made to any one aspect of the larger comparative framework without fear of misunderstanding. One might summarize the distinction between barter and sale in the classical period by saying that along every analytic axis available, the two were conventionally sundered: sale did not necessarily transfer ownership; barter did exclusively that; in sale, one could easily identify buyer and seller; in barter, not. Hence important differences arose in respect to the legal action available when one or the other party to a sale or to a barter did not follow through. In sale, non-delivery of the purchased item entitled one to a refund of monies paid. According to Paul, in barter, by contrast, if one person delivers but the other does not, the person who did not receive has an action *in personam quasi re non secuta*, "*as it were* or *as if* on the theory of non-reciprocation."[19] These efforts to insist on categorical difference – or, to pick up on the metaphor of vicinity, these efforts to insist on conceptual distance – continue into the third century, where barter is treated *ad exemplum ex empto actionis*, on analogy with the action on sale, or *vicem emptionis*, in the place of sale.[20] But in rescripts under the Tetrarchy, a change is visible: twice in that age, petitioners who gave but did not receive are granted actions for return of the object they had given *causa non secuta*.[21] It is not simply that the law had changed, barter now being treated as sale. Rather, the conceptual distance had collapsed, the need to assert *quasi* before *re non secuta* having fallen away.

To close this section, allow me to highlight important differences at the level of background or implicit understanding between the varied languages of analogy. The language of *vicinitas* is of course metaphorical: it likens conceptual or analytic similarity to geographic proximity, and so returns us to the problems of materiality and contiguity that we touched upon in chapter 1. What is more, the language of vicinity works by asserting a relationship between the things compared. (One might study the apparatus surrounding English "affinity" in the same fashion.) *Quasi*, by contrast, is about language, and all knowledge systems that rely on it: it expresses doubt about the capacity of language itself, or at the very least the capacity of the person who employs it, to give accurate and full accounting of the world with the discursive and lexical means at one's disposal. The jurists themselves theorized these issues in respect to historical change within a given society: because, one might say, *plura sunt negotia quam vocabula*, there are more things than words, the stuff of material–social relations is always escaping the reach of the law's vocabulary.[22] The problem arose so acutely at Rome because of linguistic change (as it would later in the humanist study of law): classical jurists marvelled at the self-confidence and lack of equivocation in the Twelve Tables – there are no *quasi*'s there – even as they recognized that the passage of time and changes of language and manners had rendered the language of the Twelve Tables incommensurate to the world it anteceded but still nominally ruled.[23]

Hence, for the jurists, the need for interpretation, even at Rome, which is to say, in the world that Roman law was designed to describe.

For my part, I wish to highlight the prominence of analogy and its kin in contexts in which one culture's normative language is asked to map material, social, and economic realities in a wholly different culture, which is to say, in contexts of empire.

3. I have already remarked upon Ulpian's use of substitutive *pro* to extend the scope of the law: reeds and papyrus were encompassed by the law of *lignum* by virtue of their being treated *pro ligno*, as if they were wood, although they were not. The choice to expand the scope of a law by recourse to interpretation rather than legislation is wholly unsurprising.[24] As I have said, it rests upon a recognition that it inheres in the nature of things, *in natura rerum*, that *plura sunt negotia quam vocabula*. The consequences for any normative system relying upon discursive language are clear. Even within such an understanding, however, Roman-era civil-law fictions are noteworthy, because they were routinely employed so as to permit the incorporation within the scope of existing law of things and actions that the language of the law, and the principles and taxonomies to which it gave voice, expressly did not allow. Not even Ulpian, a native of the east, was prepared to say that papyrus was in fact a type of wood: treating it as if it were was the best one was going to do. Such substitutions held their own peril, of course. Consider again Gaius's distinction between the religious and the sacred:

> That alone is thought to be sacred which is consecrated on the authority of the Roman people, either by law or by decree of the Senate. We make things *religiosum* in private actions by bearing our dead to particular sites.... But on provincial soil it is generally agreed that the soil cannot be *religiosum*, since there ownership rests with the Roman people or with Caesar, while we seem to have only possession or use. Nevertheless, even if it is not *religiosum*, it is treated as though it were (*utique tamen, etiamsi non sit religiosum, pro religioso habetur*). Similarly, whatever in the provinces is not consecrated on authority of the Roman people is properly not sacred, but it is nevertheless treated *pro sacro*, as if it were. (Gaius *Inst.* 2.5–7; the Latin text is quoted in full in chapter 1, p. 21)

In allowing that non-sacred and non-religious objects on provincial soil are appropriately treated as if they were sacred or religious, Gaius enables the regular and consistent overcoming of precisely the principles he nominally upheld – namely, the absolute reservation of authority over the sacred to the Roman people, on the one hand, and the sacral–religious distinction between Italian and provincial soil, on the other.

That said, my interest here is in the role fiction and other cognitive operations played in meeting a different demand of empire, namely, the reduplication of structures of governance through space and across varied forms of social action. I give two examples, the first a fiction, the second an abstraction.

The fiction is that of prorogation.[25] According to Livy's narrative for the year 327 BCE, the consul of that year, Quintus Publilius Philo, was on the cusp of a military victory when his term of office expired. In what seems likely to be an anachronism, Livy describes a tribune bringing a bill before the people to the effect that "when Quintus Publilius Philo should depart the consulate, he should conduct matters as if he were consul until the war with the Greeks should be successfully ended."[26] And not unexpectedly, the historian Livy's Augustan narrative finds confirmation in the Augustan *Fasti triumphales* – as Augustus commanded, so Augustan sources dutifully wrote.[27]

I translate the Latin phrase *pro consule* with the English phrase "as if he were consul," rather than with some phrase like "in the place of a consul," in order to highlight the operation of fiction in the constitutional manoeuvre.[28] To justify the claim that fiction is essential to the invention and institutionalization of prorogation, and hence to justify the translation "as if he were consul," two kinds of evidence might be cited. First, according to Livy, it remained possible as late as 187 BCE for newly elected magistrates to complain that they were being assigned duties in impoverished and unimportant areas while others, exercising power as if they were magistrates, conducted affairs in the eastern Mediterranean as private individuals.[29] The term *privati*, which I translate as "private individuals," was intended to highlight the truth of the matter, at least as the dissenters saw it, which was that the legislation that authorized prorogation was not sufficient to grant those individuals magisterial power. There had been no election and, indeed, no *lex de imperio*, no law of investiture.

The second body of evidence that we might cite to justify a translation that highlights the operation of fiction behind *prorogation* ("a procedure used in the place of putting a question to the people in assembly") is as follows. On current evidence the term *proconsul* doesn't replace the legally precise *pro consule* ("in the place of a consul") until the fall of the Republic.[30] It may have appeared in the history of Claudius Quadrigarius, but the fragment in which the term appears survives through quotation in a source of the second century CE and there is simply no guarantee that his diction was respected by that source or, for that matter, that it did not suffer alteration-*cum*-correction in transmission.[31] (The Greek term ἀνθύπατος – itself a compound from ἀνθ' + ὕπατος, meaning "in the place of the consul," where ὕπατος is a nominal form of the adjective meaning "highest" – is used in the Greek translation of Roman law on provincial commands of 101 BCE, although I observe that Michael Crawford's translation of that text back into Latin employs *pro consule*, without explanation.)[32] *Proconsul* may appear on Caesarian inscriptions – difficulties in dating preclude certainty – but I observe that the colonial charter of Urso, which was drafted between 59 and 44 BCE, still uses *pro consule*, even though the extant copy was re-inscribed under the principate.[33] The first incontrovertible instance known to me at present is found in a decree of an Augustan legate of 27 BCE.[34]

In other words, the naturalization or routinization of prorogation – of the investing of private individuals with the power of a specific magistracy without the formality of an election – took almost exactly 300 years, and it finally occurred in precisely the year in which the emperor Augustus first attempted to formalize and stabilize the holding of monarchic power *qua* aggregation of magisterial powers in a notionally democratic republic. À propos this chapter, the stabilization and routinization of the term *proconsul* represents exactly the sort of ontological commitment, manifested at the level of the lexeme, that we have already observed in the disappearance of *quasi* when the principle of nonreciprocation was cited in cases involving barter.

My second example of a mechanism employed in the reduplication of the structures of government is the prefecture. As so often in our field, something of the interest of the phenomenon in question is occluded by the existence in English of an etymological descendant of the term in question, and in translating the one with the other, the ancient term, as well as the phenomena and concepts it called to mind, are at once naturalized and effaced.

Praefectus, prefect, is the nominal form of a perfective participle, meaning "put in charge of," of which the term *praefectura*, prefecture, is an abstraction that could refer either to the office or to its bailiwick – the latter metonymic extension mirroring that of *provincia*, which is commonly understood to have as its primary meaning an administrative unit of conquered territory but which in fact referred to the bailiwick of magistrates. Like those of prefects, magistrates's spheres of responsibility could be geographically circumscribed but did not need to be so defined. At a functional level, prefects may be understood as analogues to "legates" and "vice-emperors" (there's *vice/vicem* again): each holds some power analogous to, and often derivative from, a specific power of a magistrate, who, unlike the derivative functionary, held power by virtue of election and investiture. None of these functionaries was understood to replace the magistrate in whose stead he stood: each exercised a single power only, or power radically circumscribed.

The prefecture interests me for three reasons. First, like the neuter abstractions formed from comparatives (a rare category), to wit, the correlatives *magisterium* and *ministerium*, the prefecture is capable of endless reduplication within some structure of public powers without any institutional or public-law innovation: by virtue of foregrounding the fact of being-in-charge, or the mere fact of exercising superior or subordinate power, the necessities of bureaucratic flexibility, intelligibility, and extension are prioritized over the particularity of bailiwicks. What is more, as regards the problem of empire, the nominal similarity of institutional forms from iteration to iteration is allowed to mask, and render intelligible, real diversity in the objects of institutional practice. Indeed, as regards empire and power, it is probably just this deracinated and decontextualized claim to administrative functionality, notionally distinguished from magisterial power, that made the prefecture the vehicle of choice for extending monarchic and imperial power over Rome itself. The import of this development was not lost on everyone: Suetonius recorded an anecdote, now preserved by Jerome, to the effect that Marcus Valerius Messala Corvinus, appointed the first Prefect of the City, resigned the office on the sixth day, protesting that it amounted to an "uncitizenly power."[35] To the very similar problem, namely, the elision between foreign and domestic space in the exercise of domestic powers, I will return in chapter 3.

Second, the prefecture is made visible to us in the historical record in the first instance when the need arises to extend Roman judicial administration to the region of Campania and city of Capua. The need itself arose because Capua had sided with Hannibal in the Second Punic War, and was punished by being deprived of government: to paraphrase Cicero, its senate, magistrates, and institutions of public deliberation were taken away, so that it lacked utterly the *imago rei publicae*, the very appearance of a state.[36] I have elsewhere written on the conceptual work performed when such ideal types as state or citizen were disarticulated at moments of punishment.[37] In this case, Capua was punished by disaggregating the public-law structures of government from the private-law relations of social and economic conduct among its residents. In the complex interstitial space thus created was inserted a *praefectus iure dicundo*, a man in charge of exercising jurisdiction only, a power here isolated from all other public-law powers of magistracy and functions of government, which were henceforth performed for Capua at Rome.[38]

The third reason that I focus on the prefecture is a problem of method. Much is revealed about Greece and Rome by careful study of the associative complexes activated by terms of art in their respective discursive traditions. My own sense is that in hugely important ways, those traditions remained distinct far later than is normally credited, and that the social imaginaries, the cognitive and conceptual substructures, of Greece and Rome, were powerfully different.[39] (Hence the "and" between "Greece and Rome" is in my usage disjunctive.) The term ἐπάρχω, for example, has a pedigree reaching back to Homer; the agent noun ἔπαρχος is classical but much rarer – until it becomes the standard translation for "prefect." It is on the basis of this innovation that one should study the history of the abstraction ἐπαρχεία.[40] ἐπαρχεία, like *praefectura*, can refer to the office or the bailiwick. As with tribunician power, one can speak of a prefect's ἐξουσία, the power of his office, as a thing with an ontology distinct from the holding of the office, such that the power can be granted to people who do not hold the office but function as if they did. So far as I can tell, neither the abstraction nor its metonymic reach has any parallel in the language of classical Greek public law. The reach of the term ἀρχή, for example, is very different: it can mean office or magistracy, or rulership, but it cannot refer, so far as I know, to the power of the magistracy or its bailiwick. The acts of ideation performed in Greek public law under the empire thus represent the instantiation in imperial Greek of cognitive operations imported from a Latinate thought-world.

4. In this final section, I take up one last abstraction, *civitas*, citizenship, and in so doing return to the content of chapter 1, on which I hope now to shed further light. I start by employing on *civitas* the method I have just outlined.

The obvious comparandum for *civitas* is πολιτεία.[41] But where the metonymic range of *civitas* embraces city, political community, and the territory occupied by that community, in the classical period πολιτεία never means ἄστυ, conurbation, and cannot stand for δῆμος, people or political community. In the Roman period, πολιτεία is used to translate *civitas* and so comes in the third century of this era to designate the territory of a political community (as πόλις becomes a metonym for *civitas*).[42] That πολιτεία did not interanimate δῆμος in particular in the classical period suggests that, for Greeks, juridical status is not what bound the members of a political community together. Political belonging and juridical classification were rather epiphenomenal to something else that did serve that function, namely descent or race.[43] In Rome, by contrast, juridical status, political membership, and affective belonging were assumed to map one another. This claim might be elaborated in a number of ways; here I focus on two, Roman conceptions of political identity on the one hand, and the importance of contractualism in Roman political thought on the other.

The non-existence in Latin of some term meaning "Romanness" is occasionally remarked, which doesn't stop people from using the word *Romanitas* when speaking of the classical period with some regularity.[44] To understand its absence, we might consider briefly the history of its correlate, *Latinitas*, which has two meanings: the quality or status of being Latin, and purity of speech in Latin language. When I say, "being Latin," however, I do not mean "being ethnically Latin," which is to say, being descended from one of the peoples of ancient Latium – "being Latin" is not a consequence, as Aulus Albinus once said, of being *natus in Latio*.[45] The term *Latinitas* in the usage, "the quality of being Latin," was coined in the last decades of the late Republic to refer to possession of *ius Latinum*, "the Latin right."[46]

The *ius Latinum* came into being sometime after 338 BCE. In that year, Rome declared victory in a war with the cities of Latium, and incorporated its defeated enemies into the Roman imperial state by delivering to their communities individually a set of legal rights and public-law arrangements effectively common to them all. These were initially the possession of the Latins, meaning an ethnic group with an ontology both prior to, and distinct from, the discursive apparatus of Roman imperial legal arrangements, and one could describe this package of legal rights, this *ius*, as Latin by virtue of its originary and unique association with those later called "the ancient Latins." But very shortly after 338 BCE, the Romans began to give this package of rights to communities without this ontology. The initial grantees were colonial foundations, populated largely but not exclusively by Romans and ethnic Latins. In consequence of the enrolling of indigenes in those foundations, at some moment almost undoubtedly before the end of the fourth century BCE, the Romans created people who were in our terms juridically but not ethnically Latin and ascribed the term Latin to them, which was in that moment wrenched from a realist to a nominalist usage.[47] The exact moment is now beyond recovery: the loss of Livy's text, the loss of earlier literature, and the decision by the *Thesaurus Linguae Latinae* not to write entries for proper names and adjectives, dooms any such search to failure. But by the time we can tell the history of the adjective "Latin," absent contextual information, it is no longer possible to say whether any given usage refers to peoples juridically or ethnically Latin. Nor is this surprising: as Cicero said, do you distinguish a citizen from an enemy by birth or location, or rather by mind and deed?[48]

This is not to say that neither parentage nor location of birth figured in Roman thought on political belonging. The argument of chapter 1 in respect to the place of soil and materiality in the Roman imaginary urges otherwise. But they figure only as a rare and ghostly presence in explicit theorizing on the subject, and even then obliquely. The two occasions that come to mind most readily in fact both concern language: one comes from Cicero's *Brutus*, when Atticus observes that earlier generations spoke Latin well as a rule, not because of devoted study but by virtue of not having passed their lives *extra urbem*, outside the city.[49] The other is precisely the remark of Aulus Albinus I cited a moment ago: in the preface to a work of history, he defended the quality of his prose and the composition of his work by citing his ignorance of learned technique, which he glosses as Greek. He was merely a *homo Romanus, natus in Latio*.

What the history of *Latinitas* therefore suggests is that Latin did not, in fact, lack a term to designate the quality of being Roman: what Romans shared was *civitas* or, at least once, *patria*, and likewise *civitas* apparently expressed all they shared.[50] *Romanitas* would have been tautological.

Let me now approach the topic from another angle, bringing to bear a different analytic apparatus. According to Cicero, what made someone Roman was consent to law. (As a corollary, according to the jurists, what made law was the consent of the Romans.)[51] Indeed, Cicero's claim is far more general in application, and far more specific in argument even than this. To choose only the two most famous of his many statements to this effect:

> ... populus autem non omnis hominum coetus quoquo modo congregatus, sed coetus multitudinis iuris consensu et utilitatis communione sociatus. (Cicero *Rep.* 1.39)[52]

A *populus*, a political community, is not any gathering of human beings, herded together by whatever means, but a gathering of many, joined by consent to a particular normative order and shared utility.

Quare cum lex sit civilis societatis vinculum, ius autem legis aequale, quo iure societas civium teneri potest, cum par non sit condicio civium? (Cicero *Rep.* 1.49)

Wherefore, since law is the bond of a *civilis societas*, a citizenly association, and rightful order is equivalent to law, then by what rightful order can a *societas civium*, an association of citizens be held together, when the condition of those citizens is not equal?[53]

The basic tenor of these remarks is clear enough. But to appreciate them properly, it is crucial to recognize that the terms *sociare* and *societas* are metaphorical: they are terms of art in the private law of corporations, which were, of course, purely voluntary associations.[54] (As an aside, it merits observation that here, as often in the civil law tradition, it is private law that provides intellectual resources to public-law argument.) But the specific contribution of the language of voluntary association to Ciceronian political theory should be clear: the act of joining oneself to others through shared commitment to a particular normative order was, he suggests, a purely contractual and voluntary act.[55] Chapter 3 will further explore the nature of Roman social contract theory; here let it suffice to observe that the use of *civitas* to denote both citizenship and the state at once suggests and affirms a profound reluctance to distinguish a sphere of the private apart from the normative strictures of that deemed citizenly and communal, shared, and public.

This same argument is made by Cicero ex negativo when he turns in book 3 of *De republica* to the nature of political communities under tyranny or mob rule:

Ergo illam rem populi (id est rem publicam) quis diceret tum cum crudelitate unius oppressi essent universi, neque esset unum vinculum iuris nec consensus ac societus coetus, quod est populus? (Cicero *Rep.* 3.35 Powell; translation after J. Zetzel)

So who would call that a concern of the people, that is, a commonwealth, at a time when everyone is opposed by the cruelty of a single person, when there exists neither bond of law nor shared commitment nor association of the gathered multitude, which is what is meant by *populus*, by "political community?"

An analogous argument is made, again in negative terms, when Cicero ponders the transformative effect of shared language upon aggregations of human beings (the passage is fragmentary):

[words being attached to things], [reason] gathered together humans who had previously been *dissociatos*, disjoined, and through the most pleasing bond of language tied them together. (Cicero *Rep.* 3.2 Powell)

As with the role of consent to law in creating communities from what might otherwise have been mere groups or herds, so language operates to unite individuals who had previously been nonbound by consent to its normative force. To the status of language and law as conventional, which is to say, to their status as purely products of human institution-building, I will turn in the third and final chapter.[56]

Two hundred years after Cicero, the jurist Gaius sought to explain features of the legal articulation of *collegia*, guilds, another form of voluntary association. They should be understood, he wrote, *ad exemplum rei publicae*, on analogy with a commonwealth. We witness here an act of metaphorical reversion. The explanatory direction of Cicero's argument has been reversed: the archetypal position of the voluntary association is taken by that of the political community, which the former had once explained. As we saw in chapter 1 in our study of exile and change of soil, or in this chapter in the study of barter, that which is in one era explicitly analogous and metaphorical can over time be naturalized; the need for analogy, diminished; and the status of metaphor, lost. I cannot resist quoting Nietzsche:

What, then, is truth? A mobile army of metaphors, metonyms, and anthropomorphisms – in short, a sum of human relations, which have been enhanced, transposed, and embellished poetically and rhetorically, and which after long use seem firm, canonical, and obligatory to a people: truths are illusions about which one has forgotten that this is what they are; metaphors which are worn out and without sensuous power; coins which have lost their pictures and now matter only as metal, no longer as coins.[57]

In closing this section, I turn to a passage of Livy quoted already in chapter 1, which brings together many of the themes on which I have reflected. Livy ponders the question, what would have happened to the Roman community if Brutus had attempted to liberate the people by killing an earlier king than Superbus?

Quid enim futurum fuit, si illa pastorum convenarumque plebs, transfuga ex suis populis, sub tutela inviolati templi aut libertatem aut certe impunitatem adepta, soluta regio metu agitari coepta esset tribuniciis procellis, et in aliena urbe cum patribus serere certamina, priusquam pignera coniugum ac liberorum caritasque ipsius soli, cui longo tempore adsuescitur, animos eorum consociasset? (Livy 2.1.4–5)

What would have happened if that *plebs* of shepherds and refugees, in flight from their own people, having obtained freedom or at least impunity beneath the protection of an inviolate temple, were freed from fear of a king? Would it not have begun to be agitated by tribunician dissensions and sown quarrels with the senators in a still foreign city, before their spirits had been conjoined, *consociasset*, by the tokens, the *pignora*, of wives and children and love of the soil itself, which love one inculcates only over time?

Here, the language of contract and voluntary association permeates throughout, even to the point of re-constructing one's relationship to the soil as conventional, as the product of time and socialization – though I use the term "socialization" and its cognates advisedly, they being *faux amis*, of course, but also because a major ambition of this book is to draw attention very precisely to a Roman belief in the social as institutional, as (mere) convention. Hence, I would emphasize that in so describing the love of soil, Livy highlights the extent to which, for Romans, the description of patriotic affection as springing from some biological relationship to the land itself – the description of the soil as maternal or generative – was always self-consciously metaphorical, rather than polemically natural as it was at Athens.

5. Although I have concluded by returning to a metaphor from chapter 1, by way of gesturing to chapter 3, I don't want to lose sight of the arguments specific to this chapter. I have suggested that Roman government or, to be more precise, the reduplication of the institutions of Roman government across widely heterogeneous units of rule, was made possible by, and itself promoted, particular habits of abstraction. At the level of cognitition, this occurred through taxonomic endeavours and acts of ideation that permitted the recognition of structural similarities in diverse landscapes. At the level of language, these were instantiated through abstractions that foregrounded relational rather than essentializing claims among referents and acts of synecdochic metonymy that permitted highly contingent language to regulate worlds it can scarcely have been intended to describe.

CHAPTER THREE

The Ontology of the Social

1. I quoted in chapter 1 the opening sentences of Gaius's *Institutes*, a textbook of Roman law produced in the mid-second century CE. I wish to return to that text now:

> All peoples who are governed by statutes and customs observe partly their own peculiar law and partly the common law of all human beings. The law that a people establishes for itself is peculiar to it, and is called *ius civile*, being, as it were, the special law of that *civitas*, that community of citizens, while the law that natural reason establishes among all human beings is followed by all peoples alike, and is called *ius gentium*, being, as it were, the law observed by all peoples. Thus the Roman people observes partly its own peculiar law and partly the common law of humankind.

Gaius here provides a normative account of the Roman empire's – and the world's – legal pluralism. *Iura civilia*, civil laws (to use a Roman plural that the success of Roman law rendered obsolete), are those bodies of law that every political community makes for itself. To the extent that the world is divided – and in the second century CE it remained very much divided – into separate political communities, so, on this theory, it would and should be tessellated into jurisdictions, in each of which a distinct body of law would obtain.

Pluralism is a feature of all ancient empires. Of course, at some level, along various axes all human populations are heterogeneous, but the cultural, legal, and political salience of forms of difference varies from place to place and time to time. So let me rephrase: in the ancient world, pluralism was of the essence of empire as a political form. Ancient empires, I have suggested, governed through the cultivation and management of difference. The imperial mode thus stands in distinction to the national, in which a particular culture and set of institutions is understood to penetrate, or aspires to penetrate uniformly throughout its territory and population.[1] That said, the practices by which heterogeneity was policed and sustained varied widely in the ancient world. Likewise, the anthropological awareness that rendered certain pluralisms perceptible, and the reasons that endowed those situations with normative legitimacy, were surely contingent and must have differed from place to place and time to time.

This last chapter mounts an inquiry into Roman thought in respect to the ontology of the social, with an eye towards the problematics of empire. "The ontology of the social" might seem an odd, overly abstract, excessively subtle category to be labelled a background presumption. Some such topic was only rarely the object of self-conscious theorizing in Roman antiquity. Let me explain what I mean by it, by reference to the passage of Gaius with which I began. Gaius describes the separate codes of law existing in the world as the products of human institutions. Each political society, with its own system of legislation, produces its own *ius civile*, under social, economic, demographic, political, and historical circumstances contingent to its moment of production – or moments of production – if, like the Romans, you acknowledge that legal systems evolve in irregular lockstep with changes in society at large.

What is more, Gaius offers no framework to adjudge between these codes of law, because one adheres more closely to some transcendent norm or is authorized by a source of such – god, for example; nor is any robust interest expressed here or elsewhere in texts before the Antonine Constitution in the positive law content of these separate *iura civilia*. (The Antonine Constitution is the vernacular name for the edict of the emperor Caracalla that in 212 CE granted Roman citizenship to nearly all freeborn residents of the empire.) The operative assumption would seem to be that local social orders are best secured by adherence to locally generated norms; and, as a corollary, Rome has neither an epistemic basis nor any deontological obligation to override them.[2] Certainly neither Roman lawmakers nor Roman jurists produce a normative framework for their evaluation; in the classical period, the separate systems of law of the empire at large were conceived as parallel rather than hierarchical in organization, with nary a rule of recognition operating between them.[3] By virtue of anachronistic reading the category of *ius gentium* is sometimes supposed to have supplied this want, but in classical thought *ius gentium* is understood as nothing more and nothing less than an aggregate of all those private-law norms shared between the world's separate *iura civilia*.[4] Like the categories emic and etic, *ius civile* and *ius gentium* are distinguished neither morally nor epistemologically: the latter category in both cases is the result of aggregating empirically observable phenomena. Embedded within Gaius's definition of civil law, we thus find, I argue, a typically Roman, highly relativist, radically historicized understanding of the social, undergirded by, and in turn, sustaining a remarkably narrow moral epistemology.

(As an aside, I observe that in Roman writing before the Antonine Constitution, *ius gentium* is ascribed almost no content. "All societies have slaves; Romans alone have *patria potestas*" is nearly the sum of Roman reflections on the topic, in a society that had the opportunity to know hundreds of systems of norms.[5] Roman lack of interest in the laws of others as a matter of political theory and legal anthropology, not to mention ethnography, remains a significant explanandum. Had their remarks on the topic been more robust, one might have been tempted to suggest that reflection on the non-uniformity of legal norms across known societies contributed to the moral relativism of Roman practice in regard to international private law.)

This chapter proceeds by inquiring into the place of historicism in Roman reflections on the origin of two major social institutions, law and religion. How did the practices and institutions of law and religion come to be? How, when, and why did they change? The questions are posed so as to reveal and assess a Roman commitment to constructivism in respect to the social, and thereby to consider the origin and extent of their commitment to relativism in the evaluation of the institutions of others. I focus on law and religion for the simple reason that these potentially occupy – they often do occupy, and within specific discursive traditions even at Rome, they did in fact occupy – privileged positions within particular societies' self-understandings. Legal institutions and religious practices are often the objects of divine aetiology; they are granted social authority by being credited with extra-human origins. The Romans knew many literatures in which such attributions were made; they declined to do so themselves. That is a point of difference worthy of some reflection.

As a related matter, legal and religious practice at Rome were highly formalized and, indeed, highly ritualized. They are therefore often understood even by moderns as highly fossilized: bits and pieces of the legal and religious tradition can be studied in isolation from others; each bit is traced back to some moment of origin, many bits being preserved and practised in spite of the ignorance of contemporary Romans as regards the grammar of its gestures or the meaning of its verbal components. This interpretive stance in respect to the presence of the past in various Roman presents works harm in two ways: it discourages inquiry into the ideological work performed by such engagements with pasts both real and imagined and, more crucially for me, it effaces the massive role of innovation and improvisation in legal and religious ritual. In my understanding, the discursive resources for describing innovation in the present are likely to exist – in the Roman case they did exist – in close analogical and substantive relation to the work of historical reflection in explaining invention, change, and development in the past. Hence my focus on religion and law as test cases in exploring a Roman historical self-consciousness in relation to the ontology of the social.

2. The material studied in this chapter should also be understood in relation to at least two kindred cultural phenomena that, for reasons of economy, I do not discuss at length. The first is the hugely widespread topos of Roman borrowing from others, of ideas, practices, and cultural forms, a topic that receives famous treatment by Polybius and Cicero but which is also raised by Posidonius and Diodorus among first-century BCE Greeks, as well as Sallust and Varro among Cicero's Roman contemporaries:[6]

ἃ συνιδόντες ἐμιμήσαντο ταχέως· ἀγαθοὶ γάρ, ἐι καὶ τινες ἕτεροι, μεταλαβεῖν ἔθη καὶ ζηλῶσαι τὸ βέλτιον καὶ Ῥωμαῖοι. (Polybius 6.25.11)

Perceiving these things (about Greek arms), they swiftly copied them, for the Romans are good in this respect, too – if indeed there are others good in this way – that they change customs and imitate what is better.

Atqui multo id facilius cognosces, inquit Africanus, si progredientem rem publicam atque in optimum statum naturali quodam itinere et cursu venientem videris; quin hoc ipso sapientiam maiorum statues esse laudandam, quod multa intelleges etiam aliunde sumta meliora apud nos multo esse facta, quam ibi fuissent, unde huc translata essent atque ubi primum extitissent, intellegesque non fortuito populum Romanum, sed consilio et disciplina confirmatum esse nec tamen adversante fortuna. (Cicero *Rep.* 2.30; trans. Zetzel)

In fact you will recognize that even more clearly, said Africanus, if you watch the commonwealth improving and approaching the ideal constitution by a natural route and direction; you will decide that this is itself a reason to praise our ancestors' wisdom, because you will recognize how much better they made the institutions borrowed from other places than they had been in the place of origin from which we adopted them; you will see that the Roman people grew strong not by chance but by planning and discipline, if not without some help from fortune.

Against a backdrop of Greek historical reflection-*cum*-fundamentalism, in which laws, cloaked in some native purity, were delivered to communities all at once by a lawgiver, or rites were instituted at some originary, epiphanic moment, and the only conceivable social movements are a falling away or clawing back, Roman openness at once to change and influence from non-Roman sources remains a stunning point of difference.[7] To the specific topic of the origins of law and the impetus for and sources of its evolution in Roman thought, we will turn in a moment.

The second phenomenon lying in the background of the material studied in this chapter is the banal but not unimportant use made by select Roman intellectuals of Greek natural law theory (banal in part because the theory itself is puerile): it is cited in philosophizing asides by various Roman theorists, when they wish to contrast the contingent, fallible, bounded, and particularist nature of any given law or law code, over against the ontologically elevated status of nature or right reason, which is then denominated in such texts also as law with a capital "L." The most sustained engagement with Greek natural law theory in a Roman text is found in the first book of Cicero's *De Legibus*, where two strands of the argument have relevance here. First, it is affirmed that in contrast with some universal law, which is apparently transparently intelligible (if not practised), the laws of one's own state, written in one's own language, require jurists for their intrepretation. This results at least in part from the fact that laws find articulation in discursive language, and languages are contingent not only from culture to culture, but from time to time.[8] The second point follows from this, to wit, that it is crucial to distinguish the quite separate tasks of inquiring into universal law or the law of nature or what have you, and the legislation by which communities ought to be governed, on the one hand, and exploring the "laws and decrees of peoples as they are in fact composed and written," on the other. Among the many bodies of positive law that one might study, Cicero avers, are the "so-called civil laws" of Rome.[9] If here it is merely implied that Roman law has no necessary claim to ethical or moral superiority over any other body of law, that point is made explicitly in Cicero's *De re publica*, where Roman law is named alongside Athenian law as examples of norms that will be transcended in some eschatological future when the rule of natural law is realized on earth.[10] Cicero's musings notwithstanding, this tradition had stunningly little effect in later Roman legal theory, where a wholly different and vastly more fascinating concept of nature dominated. To it, too, we will return.

3. In what follows I proceed fairly schematically and explore first in legal sources four topics: accounts of the origins of law; explanations of the circumstances of change in the law; the institutional mechanisms for effecting and authorizing change; and the discursive means available within the legal tradition for explaining change in relation to earlier norms. I will then pursue the same topics in turn in a reading of religious texts, though

generic differences will mean that the comparison can rarely be exact.

Although historical reflection occupies a central place in Roman legal thought, it has been little studied and the evidence has never been assembled. The obvious point of departure (but by no means the only relevant text) is the *Handbook* of Pomponius, whose history of Roman law is excerpted in the opening book of the *Digest*. Consider the following extracts (Pomponius *Encheiridion* fr. 178 Lenel = *Dig*. 1.2.2.*pr*.–2, 7–8, 11, 48 [trans. de Ste. Croix]):

(pr.) Necessarium itaque nobis videtur ipsius iuris originem atque processum demonstrare. (1) Et quidem initio civitatis nostrae populus sine lege certa, sine iure certo primum agere instituit omniaque manu a regibus gubernabantur. (2) Postea **aucta ad aliquem modum civitate** ipsum Romulum traditur populum in triginta partes divisisse, quas partes curias appellavit propterea quod tunc reipublicae curam per sententias partium earum expediebat: et ita leges quasdam et ipse curiatas ad populum tulit: tulerunt et sequentes reges.

Accordingly, it seems that we must account for the origin and development of law itself. (1) The fact is that at the outset of our *civitas*, the *populus* decided to conduct its affairs without fixed statute law or determinate legal rights; everything was governed by the kings by their own hand. (2) **When the *civitas* subsequently grew to a reasonable size**, then Romulus himself, according to the tradition, divided the citizen body into thirty parts and called them *curiae* on the grounds that he improved his curatorship of the commonwealth (*reipublicae curam*) through the advice of these parts. And accordingly, he himself enacted for the people a number of statutes passed by advice of the *curiae*; his successors legislated likewise.

(7) **augescente civitate quia deerant quaedam genera agendi**, non post multum temporis spatium Sextus Aelius alias actiones composuit et librum populo dedit, qui appellatur ius aelianum. (8) Deinde cum esset in civitate lex duodecim tabularum et ius civile, essent et legis actiones, evenit, ut plebs in discordiam cum patribus perveniret et secederet sibique iura constitueret, quae iura plebi scita vocantur.

(7) **With the city growing, because some types of legal action were found to be lacking**, Sextus Aelius not much later composed further forms of action and gave to the people the book that is called "The Law according to Aelius." (8) Then, since in the *civitas* there was the statute law of the 12 Tables, and on top of that there was the *ius civile*, and on top of that the *legis actiones*, it came to pass that the *plebs* fell at odds with the members of the senatorial class and seceded and set up laws for itself, which laws are called plebiscites.

(11) Novissime sicut ad pauciores iuris constituendi vias transisse **ipsis rebus dictantibus** videbatur per partes, evenit, ut necesse esset rei publicae per unum consuli (nam senatus non perinde omnes provincias probe gerere poterant): igitur constituto principe datum est ei ius, ut quod constituisset, ratum esset.

Most recently, just as there was seen to have been a transition toward fewer ways of establishing law, a transition effected by stages **as circumstances themselves dictated**, it has come about that affairs of state have had to be entrusted to one man (for the senate had been unable latterly to govern all the provinces honestly). An emperor having been appointed, to him was given the right that what he had decided be deemed law.

(27) Cumque consules avocarentur bellis finitimis neque esset qui in civitate ius reddere posset, factum est, ut praetor quoque crearetur, qui urbanus appellatus est, quod in urbe ius redderet.

And since the consuls were being called away to wars with neighboring peoples and there was no one who was empowered to attend to legal business in the political community, it was accomplished that a praetor, too, was created, who was called "the urban praetor," because he attended to legal business in the city.

(32) Capta deinde Sardinia mox Sicilia, item Hispania, deinde Narbonensi provincia totidem praetores, quot provinciae in dicionem venerant, creati sunt, partim qui urbanis rebus, partim qui provincialibus praeessent.

Sardinia then being annexed, and soon Sicily, and likewise Hispania, and later Narbonensis, as many praetors were created as provinces came under Roman control, some of whom supervised urban and some provincial affairs.

(48) Et ita Ateio Capitoni Massurius Sabinus successit, Labeoni Nerva, qui adhuc eas dissensiones auxerunt. hic etiam Nerva Caesari familiarissimus fuit. Massurius Sabinus in equestri ordine fuit et publice primus respondit: posteaque hoc coepit beneficium dari, a Tiberio Caesare hoc tamen illi concessum erat.

And so when Ateius Capito was succeeded by Masurius Sabinus, and Labeo by Nerva, these two increased the above-mentioned range of disagreements. Nerva was also on the most intimate terms with Caesar. Massurius Sabinus was of equestrian rank and was the first person to give state-authorized opinions. For after this privilege began to be given, it was granted to him by Tiberius Caesar.

Let me draw your attention to five features of Pomponius' account:

- Although the opening sentence of his text might seem to suggest that the "origin of law itself" is chronologically prior to, or perhaps transcends, the foundation of the Roman community, the origin of law not only postdates the mere aggregation of persons under royal rule, but occurs in consequence of the political articulation of the people as a community of citizens capable of deliberation and self-rule. We see identical claims in respect to the historical ontology of law in a fragment of Gaius's commentary on the Twelve Tables, where he insists a history of law must begin *ab urbis initiis*, "from the foundation of the city,"[11] and also in Lucretius *De rerum natura* book 5, where it is kings who found cities but it is only after they are expelled that humans learn to create magistrates and establish laws.[12]
- Legal change is indexed to social change, and social change in turn to demographic change: (2) "When the *civitas* subsequently grew to a reasonable size" (*acta ad aliquem modum civitate*), (7) "With the city growing, because some types of legal action were found to be lacking ..." (*augescente civitate quia deerant quaedam genera agendi*).

- At the same time, change is understood at once to be incremental and driven by factors exogenous to the institutions of legal deliberation; nor is agency in legal change articulated through some cult of personality: (11) "just as there was seen to have been a transition toward fewer ways of establishing law, a transition effected by stages as circumstances themselves dictated …"
- Pomponius writes as if the creation of more praetors to exercise domestic power at Rome, because of exogenous demands on the machinery of the state (27), and the creation of more praetors to exercise imperial power over non-citizens, because the empire had grown (32), were politically and ideologically similar operations (*partim … partim* [32]). By his day, apparently no particular distinction needed to be drawn in such a context between governing Romans and governing others.
- Finally (48), at every stage the positive content of statute law is the object of disagreement and its texts subject to interpretive disagreements, as well as disagreements about interpretive method.

These varied themes find articulation elsewhere in legal theory and statute law. The jurists discuss these issues most prominently when reflecting on the legal pluralism of the Roman legal system, meaning in this case the simultaneous operation at Rome of multiple sources of law. For example, Papinian describes the law as articulated by magistrates charged with jurisdiction as "that which in the public interest those magistrates, the praetors, have introduce in aid or supplementation or correction of statute law" (*Ius praetorium est, quod praetores introduxerunt adiuuandi vel supplendi vel corrigendi iuris civilis gratia propter utilitatem publicam*).[13]

That said, neither newer sources of law, nor new laws, were understood at Rome as necessarily superseding earlier sources of law, or earlier statute. As regards statute, consider the remarkable text of the Neronian law on customs of Asia.[14] After a preface dating from its (re)publication in 62 CE, the inscribed copy contains what is apparently the original text, followed by a chronologically ordered summary of revisions. These are introduced by the names of the consuls in office when the revisions were introduced. At any given instance of the law's re-enactment, some content was thus tralatician, some not:

(84) Λούκιος Γέλλιος, Γναῖος Λέντλος ὕπατοι προσέθηκαν·

The consuls Lucius Gellius and Gnaeus Lentulus added: (72 BCE)

(88) Γάϊος Φούρνιος, Γάϊος Σειλανὸς ὕπατοι προσέθηκαν·

The consuls Gaius Furnius and Gaius Silanus added: (17 BCE)

(103-4) Πόπλιος Σουλπίκιος Κουιεῖνος, Λούκιος Οὐάλγιος | [Ροῦφος ὕπατοι πρ]οσέθηκαν·]

[The consuls] Publius Sulpius Quirin<i>us and Lucius [*sic*] Valgius [Rufus] added: (12 BCE)

(138–9) Σεβα]στὸς ὕπατος προσέθηκεν· ὃς ἂν ταύτην τὴν δημοσιωίαν μισθώσηται, οὗτος τούτωι τῶι νόμωι | [καὶ τούτοις τοῖς κεφαλαίοις (?) χρώμενος αὐτὴν] τὴν μεμισθωμένην ἔθεσιν ἑξῆς πέντε καρπεύεσθαι ὀφειλέτω· **τὰ λοιπὰ κατὰ τὸν αὐτὸν νόμον**.

The consul Tiberius Claudius Caesar Augustus added: whoever has accepted the contract for this *vectigal*, he is to be obliged to exploit [it], once it has been accepted for five years in succession, [obeying] this *lex* [and these chapters (?);] the rest (is to be) according to the same *lex*. (42 or 43 CE)

As the wording of the law's protocols makes clear, the new material at each enactment did not supersede or replace the old wholesale: clauses were added, which might entail a revision or effacement of some clauses from earlier enactments. The overall relationship of the new to the old is clarified in the somewhat more expansive formula used for the changes introduced in 42/43 CE (lines 138–9): "The consul Tiberius Claudius Caesar Augustus added ... The rest is to be according to the same *lex*." Even the single statute governing the customs duties for goods moving in and out of the province of Asia is the product of a complex and ongoing historical imbrication. How much more the law in its totality?

Public law – what an American might call constitutional law – constitutes a case unto itself as a substantive matter, one so famous as to require no elaboration. But it perhaps bears mentioning that, as with citizenship and openness to cultural borrowing more generally, so in public law, the incremental nature of change in Roman constitutional law in response to contingencies of every kind was an object of comparative reflection by both Greeks and Romans. In the words of the Augustan critic and historian Dionysius of Halicarnassus:

> And in the course of time they contrived to raise themselves from the smallest nation to the greatest and from the most obscure to the most illustrious, not only by their humane reception of those who sought a home among them, but also by sharing the rights of citizenship with all who had been conquered by them in war after a brave resistance, by permitting all the slaves, too, who were manumitted among them to become citizens, and by disdaining no condition of men from whom the commonwealth might reap an advantage, but above everything else by their form of government, which they fashioned out of their many experiences, always extracting something useful from every occasion (ὑπὲρ ταῦτα δὲ πάντα κόσμῳ τοῦ πολιτεύματος, ὃν ἐκ πολλῶν κατεστήσαντο παθημάτων, ἐκ παντὸς καιροῦ λαμβάνοντές τι χρήσιμον). (Dionysius of Halicarnassus *Roman Antiquities* 1.9.4)

The same topic is subject to ironic play in Cicero's *Republic*, where Laelius criticizes Scipio for producing a Hellenizing narrative: he had rehearsed a history of Roman government in which kings-qua-legislators established and revised institutions, thereby ascribing to transcendant acts of reason developments that had actually occurred *casu aut necessitate*, in response to chance or necessity.[15]

Alongside these patterns in historical self-consciousness lies another, regarding the power of legal language to shape the social reality that it nominally describes and regulates. Consider, for example, the interpretation given by Cicero of a clause in a proposed agrarian law of 63 BCE. The law proposed the creation of special magistrates to carry out its enactments, but those magistrates would have to be authorized by a separate law, which might of course not pass. The proposed statute itself employed an exhortative to work around this problem: if the law authorizing the magistrates does not pass, the first law nonetheless simply declares them to have the power of those who are properly authorized. (Elsewhere, as we shall see, secular and religious texts tend to use third-person imperatives.)

Quid postea, si ea lata non erit? Attendite ingenium. "Tvm ei xviri," inquit, "eodem ivre sint qvo qvi optima lege." Si hoc fieri potest ut in hac civitate quae longe iure libertatis ceteris civitatibus antecellit quisquam nullis comitiis imperium aut potestatem adsequi possit, quid attinet tertio capite legem curiatam ferre iubere, cum quarto permittas ut sine lege curiata idem iuris habeant quod haberent, si optima lege a populo essent creati? (Cicero *Contra Rullum* 2.29)

What then, if the *lex* is not passed? Note his ingenuity! "Then let the decemvirs be of the same legal standing as those created according to strict procedure." If this is indeed possible, that in this polity, which excels all other polities by far in the rights of liberty, someone should be able to obtain command over citizens or administrative authority without the authorization of any electoral body, what is the point of ordering the passage of a curiate law in the third chapter, when in the fourth you permit that these officials should have the same legal status without a curiate law as they would have had if they had been created by the people according to strict procedure?

Observe that Cicero offers two representations of the law: the first purports to use the actual wording of the proposed legislation; that is where we find the exhortative, creating a new legal reality in revision of a social reality that had failed to comply. In Cicero's restatement, this work is performed by a legal fiction: the magistrates created by the agrarian law are to have "the same legal status without a curiate law as they would have had if they had been created according to strict procedure." Please observe that the fiction does not deny or invalidate the principle that magistrates should be authorized by a separate curiate law. Indeed, one might say it genuflects before it. The fiction is rather of the successful performance of the action that would have concretized the principle, had it occurred at all.[16]

As an aside, let me point out that a similar schizophrenia in regard to the validity of the past in the present that both honours and revises it is visible at a purely formal level in the genres of jurisprudential scholarship at Rome. On the one hand, the conservatism of the jurists in respect to the sources of law in their own tradition is perhaps best marked by their near absolute devotion to the lemmatic commentary as a literary form; while on the other, the very contemporaneity and comprehensiveness of juristic writing led to the gradual elision from their texts of the very words upon which they commented. In other words, as each new generation of jurists wrote commentaries on earlier commentaries on statute law, they gradually ceased to quote the original words of the statute, which receded ever farther into the past. Those words were clearly understood to remain in some way dispositive, but only via acts of interpretation that enabled their language to map present-day social conduct, which had itself been adapted to meet the requirements of law as then understood. To cite a related reflection of the jurist Tertullian, "Because it is common practice to read earlier laws in light of later ones, one ought always to believe *as if* it inheres in laws that they pertain to persons and things that will someday be similar."[17] In this way, the ultimate sources of law in the classical period were both honoured and effaced.

One result of the continual operation of these work-arounds in legal practice was the development in Roman legal theory of a remarkable distinction between legal facts and social reality, as well as a recognition that the former operates to alter the latter largely through the consensual commitment of those governed by the law to accept its decisions as legitimate – as pure a statement of Rawlsian constructivism as one might wish. The gap thereby opened up between the world created by the law and some other reality is nonetheless consistently marked by Roman jurists. Consider, for example, the original context of Ulpian's famous obiter dictum, "legal decisions are accepted in the place of truth"

(Ulpian *Lex Iulia et Papia* bk. 1 frag. 1978 Lenel = *Dig.* 1.5.25 (also, in part, 50.17.207) & *Dig.* 40.16.4 & *Dig.* 40.10.6):

Ingenuum accipere debemus etiam eum, de quo sententia lata est, quamvis fuerit libertinus: quia res iudicata pro veritate accipitur.

We must accept as freeborn someone concerning whom there is a judgment to that effect, even if he was born a freedman: for legal decisions are accepted in the place of truth.

Si libertinus per collusionem fuerit pronuntiatus ingenuus, collusione detecta in quibus causis quasi libertinus incipit esse. medio tamen tempore, antequam collusio detegatur et post sententiam de ingenuitate latam, utique quasi ingenuus accipitur. Libertinus si ius anulorum impetraverit, quamvis iura ingenuitatis salvo iure patroni nactus sit, tamen ingenuus intellegitur: et hoc divus hadrianus rescripsit.

If a freedman has through collusion been pronounced of free birth and the collusion is discovered, from that time he is treated as if a freedman in all respects. Nonetheless, in the intervening time after the judgment for free birth and before discovery of the collusion, he is certainly taken to be as if free born. If a freedman has sought and obtained the right to rings, although he has acquired the rights of free birth – his patron's rights being protected – nonetheless he is understood as a freeborn person: so the divine Hadrian ruled by rescript.

In the abstract, the question before Ulpian is how to navigate as a matter of theory and language the discrepant worlds of social and legal facts, the former being created by the actual life histories of the parties involved, which the legal system both understands in light of normative categories and itself revises. Beyond the potential for error inherent in any regulatory system, Ulpian confronts here the possibilities of deceit and successive revision. In his solution, we witness an ongoing emphasis upon the nominalism of legal language: the terms *quasi libertinus* and *quasi ingenuus* flag Ulpian's awareness that, his own principle notwithstanding, the person created by the law as freeborn in contravention of his status in historical–social reality is an epistemic and linguistic *monstrum*.

Several decades before Ulpian, Gaius had confronted a similar problem in his consideration of the law of theft.[18] A statute established that refusing to allow one's property to be searched for stolen goods rendered one liable for the action against manifest theft. (Merely being caught with stolen goods made one liable for a lesser degree of theft.) This caused some writers to ask whether theft was manifest *aut lege aut natura*, "by statute or in reality." That is to say, was manifest theft a particular form of theft, or could any act of theft be not merely classified as, but in fact transformed into manifest theft through statutory language?

Propter hoc tamen, quod lex ex ea causa manifestum furtum esse iubet, sunt, qui scribunt furtum manifestum aut lege intellegi aut natura: lege id ipsum, de quo loquimur, natura illud, de quo superius exposuimus. sed verius est natura tantum manifestum furtum intellegi; neque enim lex facere potest, ut qui manifestus fur non sit, manifestus sit, non magis quam qui omnino fur non sit, fur sit, et qui adulter aut homicida non sit, adulter vel homicida sit; at illud sane lex facere potest, ut **proinde** aliquis poena teneatur, **atque si** furtum vel adulterium vel homicidium admisisset, quamvis nihil eorum admiserit.

Nevertheless, because of this, namely, that the statute orders that in such cases the theft be manifest, there are those who will say that theft may be understood to be manifest on the basis of statute or in reality: by statute in the situation we are now discussing, and in reality in the circumstance we described above. The truer answer is that manifest theft is understood as manifest on the basis of reality. For statute can no more bring it about that a non-manifest thief is manifest, than it can make someone who is altogether not a thief into a thief, or someone who is not an adulterer or a homicide into an adulterer or a homicide. Rather, what law can do is simply this, it can make someone liable to punishment exactly as if he had committed theft or adultery or homicide, even if he had committed none of those things. (Gaius *Inst.* 3.194; translation after du Zulueta)

Gaius responds by erecting a firewall between some lived social reality that he denominates *natura* and the world created by fallible legal institutions. This "nature" is not somehow divorced from the world of human beings by virtue of being non-domesticated or uninhabited, to situate it along two polarities elsewhere operative in ancient thought; nor is nature divinely created and so free from human error, a place closer to paradise or of greater immanence of right reason. It is, rather, the lived reality of humans in the world, who create for themselves rules and institutions to regulate their affairs, to which they assign a certain authority and narrowly normative transcendence but which they also endow with their own very human moral and epistemic limitations.[19]

4. I turn now to thought and action in the domain of religion, and I proceed in reverse order relative to what I have observed in regard to law, which is to say, I commence with the forms and justification of innovation in the present and only later study the historical self-consciousness operative in religious texts.

In ritual as in the law, ad hoc innovation is understood to take place *ipsis rebus dictantibus*, "as circumstances themselves dictated," and innovation in ritual was understood also to work through substitition. Such in any event is the principle cited by Servius as operative whenever one lacks the item normatively called for in religious ritual:

VIRGINE CAESA non vere, sed ut videbatur. et sciendum in sacris simulata pro veris accipi: unde cum de animalibus quae difficile inveniuntur est sacrificandum, de pane vel cera fiunt et pro veris accipiuntur. (Servius *ad Aen.* 2.116)

THE MAIDEN KILLED: not truly, but in seeming. Indeed, one should know that in rites the pretend is taken for the true: whence, when it is necessary to sacrifice an animal but they are hard to find, the sacrifice is made from bread or wax and these are accepted in the place of the true.

Servius of course speaks of sacrifice, and of human sacrifice to boot: one might therefore be suspicious that the principle is an interested one, invented to explain away a literary–mythological moment. But similar language in respect to vegetal sacrifice was wholly traditional, and indeed was also employed for the instruments of ritual and not just offerings.[20]

Again, in religious as in secular law, there was a pressing need to craft some framework to bridge the gap between actions performed *optima lege*, according to strict procedure (to use Cicero's language), and those not so performed. In so doing, often enough actions taken outside statal control were granted the legitimacy of public authorities, but by the same means they were subsumed under the normative framework and notional supervision of those same authorities. One could cite as an example the assimilation of non-Roman actions to Roman taxonomies of the sacred in Gaius's *Institutes*, which we read already in chapter 2:

> That alone is thought to be sacred, which is consecrated on the authority of the Roman people, either by law or by decree of the Senate. We make things *religiosum* in private actions by bearing our dead to particular sites.... But on provincial soil it is generally agreed that the soil cannot be *religiosum*, since there ownership rests with the Roman people or with Caesar, while we seem to have only possession or use. Nevertheless, even if it is not *religiosum*, it is treated as though it were. Similarly, whatever in the provinces is not consecrated on authority of the Roman people is properly not sacred, but it is nevertheless treated *pro sacro*, as if it were. (Gaius *Inst*. 2.5–7)

A modern reader might well ask whether Gaius has not effectively undermined the principle articulated by Trajan in a famous response to Pliny, "the method of consecration being different from that practised among us," Pliny could proceed without scruple, "as the soil of an alien city cannot receive consecration as it is performed according to our law." What was the difference in practice between holding provincial land sacred, on the one hand, and holding it non-sacred but treating it as though it were, on the other? And if there were no difference in practice, would that not undermine the purely theoretical distinction operative in legal principle? On the contrary, Gaius and the jurists understood fiction and substitution as preeminently conservative devices, precisely because they left the normative commitments of earlier law unrevised.

Again, as in the agrarian law proposed by Rullus, so in religion the creation of religious legal facts occurs through the use of third-person imperatives. This phenomenon of Roman religious language was the object of a famous study by Arthur Darby Nock, who commenced with the language of the vow of a sacred spring in 217 BCE:[21]

... Qui faciet, quando volet quaque lege volet facito; quo modo faxit probe factum esto. Si id moritur quod fieri oportebit, profanum esto, neque scelus esto. Si quis rumpet occidetve insciens, ne fraus esto. Si quis clepsit, ne populo scelus esto neue cui cleptum erit. Si atro die faxit insciens, probe factum esto. Si nocte sive luce, si servus sive liber faxit, probe factum esto. Si antidea senatus populusque iusserit fieri ac faxitur, eo populus solutus liber esto. (Livy 22.10.2–6)

Let him who performs the sacrifice do so whenever he wants, by whatever rite; however he shall do it, let it be considered to have been done properly. If something intended for sacrifice should die, let it be held profane and let it be understood that no crime has taken place. If someone should steal <the object intended for sacrifice>, let no blame attach to the people nor to the person from whom it was stolen. If he should unwittingly perform the sacrifice on an inappropriate day, let the sacrifice be considered to have been done properly. If by night or day, if slave or free should perform the sacrifice, let be held to have been done properly. If the sacrifice shall be performed on the day before the Senate and People order it to be performed, let the people be held free and absolved from it.

Notably, to follow on the Rawlsian perspective that I adopted earlier, the language of the vow is held binding on the community united by the normative framework that it instantiates, a community that includes the gods.

Furthermore, as in Cicero's interpretation of the agrarian law, so in religious law the work of third-person imperatives could be assimilated to the work of fiction. Consider, for example, the *lex sacra* or sacred law of the cult of Jupiter at Furfo (*CIL* I² 756 = *AÉ* 2008, 56, ll. 7–10, 12–14; I adapt the edition and translation of Tamás Adamik):[22]

(7–10) Sei quod ad eam aedem donum datum donatum dedicatum que erit, utei liceat oeti venum dare; ubei venum datum erit, id profanum esto. Venditio locatio aedilis esto, quemquomque veicus Furfensis fecerint, quod se sentiunt eam rem sine scelere sine piaculo; alis non potesto.

If something shall be given, donated or dedicated as a gift at this temple, let it be permitted to use or sell [that thing]; when it shall have been been sold, let it be profane. The sale or leasing shall be up to the aedile, whomsoever the village of Furfo shall create, so far as they feel that they are willing, without impiety or guilt; no one else shall be able to.

(12–14) Quod emptum erit aere aut argento ea pequnia quae pecunia ad id templum data erit, quod emptum erit, eis rebus eadem lex esto quasei sei dedicatum sit.

What shall have been bought with bronze or silver, for that money which money shall have been given to this temple, what will have been bought, to those things the same regulation is to apply as if they had been dedicated.

Objects given or dedicated at a temple became sacred and were henceforth the property of the god to whom the temple was dedicated. As a matter of law, they were placed beyond human ownership and outside the possibility of economic exchange, nor could they be released or sold unless subjected to a rite of desacralization and hence rendered profane. Likewise, those objects purchased for use on temple property, like the property itself, were *stricto sensu* the property of the god and thus sacred. Reading these clauses against that background, we may say that in the first clause, a legal religious fact is asserted to follow even upon the non-performance of the rite of desacralization, though the non-performance of the ritual is itself not cited. Rather, the effect of the rite is created through the operation of legal language alone: *id profanum esto*, "let it be profane." In the second clause, a kindred action is explicitly said to rest upon the fiction of a ritual's performance.

5. I turn now to some Roman accounts of specific historical changes.

In 209 BCE, a newly appointed *flamen Dialis*, which is to say, a newly appointed priest of Jupiter, one Gaius Valerius, attempted to claim a seat in the Senate *ex officio*. Livy describes both the opposition that this aroused and the form of the debate that followed:

Ingressum eum curiam cum P. Licinius praetor inde eduxisset, tribunos plebis appellavit. Flamen vetustum ius sacerdotii repetebat: datum id cum toga praetexta et sella curuli ei flamonio esse. Praetor non exoletis uetustate annalium exemplis stare ius, sed recentissimae cuiusque consuetudinis usu volebat: nec patrum nec avorum memoria Dialem quemquam id ius usurpasse. (Livy 27.8.8–9)

After Flaccus had entered the Senate, Publius Licinius the praetor escorted him out. Flaccus appealed to the tribunes of the plebs. The *flamen* sought an ancient right of the priesthood: [entry to the Senate] had been granted to the flaminate together with the *toga praetexta* and *sella curulis*. The praetor wanted privileges to rest not upon historical examples of tiresome antiquity, but in each case upon the most recent practice: not in the memory of their fathers or grandfathers (i.e., not in the two immediate prior generations) had any *flamen Dialis* vindicated that right.

The praetor who opposed Flaccus's request urged that privileges should rest "not upon historical examples of tiresome antiquity, but in each case upon the most recent practice." That is to say, it was wholly conceivable at Rome to argue that in a matter of religious law, the most recent (and most directly analogous) precedent should be dispositive, over against some claim to ancientness or originalism. Mutatis mutandis, in the conduct of ritual, it is the most recent successful performance that is taken as paradigmatic. That performance might be ancient, or it might have recreated some first performance, but that would be a contingent fact regarding that particular rite, not a generalizable argument on behalf of ancientness or originalism in themselves. It is for this reason that I have argued that Livy's narrative might function at Rome as a form of aetiological myth. For he often describes not only the first performance of a ritual, but subsequent performances, and also, occasionally, modifications on the occasion of those later performances, and it was the most recent successful performance – or even, the principles articulated and actualized in that performance – that one had to recreate in future performance at Rome.[23]

In this context it is tempting to cite the clause attributed in the first century BCE to the Twelve Tables of the mid-fifth century BCE, which purported to offer a decision-rule in cases of conflicts of law:

in XII tabulas legem esse, ut quodcumque postremum populus iussisset, id ius ratumque esset. (Livy 7.17.12)[24]

... it was enacted in the Twelve Tables that whatsoever the people decreed most recently, that should be law and binding.

My object here is not to debate the veracity of the text as a piece of early Roman legislation. Rather, I cite this text as an example of a serious claim of legal principle, repeatedly advanced in different forms and various *fora* in the late Republic. It has a close kindred in another claim of principle advanced elsewhere in Livy, to the effect that "where two laws are in conflict, the newer always abrogates the older."[25] For students of Roman culture, accustomed to motivated invocations of ancestral custom, these texts might seem outlandish, to be taken as outliers. But the text of the customs law of Asia accords completely with these principles, and many other examples from law might be cited.

In consequence of this attitude to the status of the past in explaining the present, the Romans understood change in ritual practice to have occurred with regular irregularity, to have occurred through human agency, and to have been authorized above all by human law-making. Consider, for example, the catalogue of changes and alterations to rites (*permutationes* and *emendationes sacrificiorum*) compiled in book 1 of Macrobius's *Saturnalia*:

[Praetextatus:] "I also find it recorded that when many men used the occasion of the Saturnalia to extort gifts from clients out of greedy self-interest, so that the less well off were burdened, Publicius, a tribune of the plebs, carried a measure forbidding anything but candles to be sent to the wealthy."

Here Caecina Albinus interposed: "The sort of change in sacrifice that you mentioned just now, Praetextatus (*Qualem nunc permutationem sacrificii, Praetextate, memorasti*), I find to have been observed later in the case of the Compitalia, when the games used to be celebrated at the crossroads throughout the city, after Tarquin the Proud reestablished them in honor of the Lares and the Mania, in accordance with an oracle of Apollo directing that the gods' favour be sought 'with heads on behalf of heads.' For some time it was the practice of sacrificing children to Mania, mother of the Lares, to assure the well-being of household members. After the expulsion of Tarquin, the consul Junius Brutus decided that the sacrifice should be celebrated differently (*aliter*), ordering that the gods' favour be sought with heads of garlic and poppy: that way the terms of Apollo's oracle stipulating 'heads' could be satisfied, while the crime attaching to the ill-omened sacrifice would be avoided. So it came to be that likenesses of Mania hung before each household's door to avert any danger that might threaten the household's members, and the games themselves came to be called the Compitalia, from the crossroads in which they were celebrated. But please do complete your account."

Praetextatus said: "Your account of that similar correction of ritual practice was well timed...." (*Bene et oportune similis emendatio sacrificiorum relata est*) (Macrobius *Saturnalia* 1.7.34–6; trans. Kaster)

Macrobius catalogues changes made to the Saturnalia itself and also to the Compitalia, in the former case by "Publicius the tribune" and in the latter by Iunius Brutus. (I observe that the latter change is a substitution, of heads of garlic and poppy for heads of persons, and is justified through an act of interpretation.) In neither case is the reform or change in question motivated by an omen or a verbal command from a deity, nor is either a wholesale revision of the rite: in the words of the customs law of Asia, "the rest is to be according to the same *lex*."

What is more, as was at stake in Cicero's contestation of the fiction in Rullus's agrarian law, new ritual forms, which is to say, revised ritual forms are held to be efficacious even when they might seem to violate some principle inherent in earlier practice. Consider, for example, two accounts of changes to the religious and legal rituals by which Romans understood themselves to settle disputes over property, on the one hand, and to have declared war, on the other:[26]

Correptio manus in re atque in loco praesenti apud praetorem ex duodecim tabulis fiebat, in quibus ita scriptum est: si qui in iure manum conserunt. Sed postquam praetores, **propagatis Italiae finibus**, satis iurisdictionis negotiis occupati, proficisci vindiciarum dicendarum causa ad longinquas res gravabantur, institutum est **contra duodecim tabulas** tacito consensu, ut litigantes non in iure apud praetorem manum consererent, sed "ex iure manum consertum" vocarent, id est alter alterum ex iure ad conserendam manum in rem de qua ageretur vocaret atque profecti simul in agrum de quo litigabatur, terrae aliquid ex eo, uti unam glebam, in ius in urbem ad praetorem deferrent et in ea gleba **tamquam** in toto agro vindicarent. (Gellius 20.10.9)

According to the Twelve Tables, a seizure by hand of thing or place took place in the presence of the praetor. For there it is written, "If any lay on hands in court...." But later, **after the boundaries of Italy were extended**, the praetors became preoccupied by legal matters and were reluctant to travel for the sake of hearing claims to far-off objects. As a result, it was decided by tacit agreement, **contrary to the Twelve Tables**, that litigants would not lay on hands in court before the praetor, but they would call for "a laying-on of hands according to the law." That is, one litigant would summon the other to the disputed object for a laying-on of hands in accordance with the law. Having set out at the same time to the field in question, they would bear back from it some bit of earth – a clod, for example – to the city, into court before the praetor and on that clod, **as if** on the whole field they would speak their claim.

PRINCIPIUM PUGNAE hoc de Romana sollemnitate tractum est. cum enim volebant bellum indicere, pater patratus, hoc est princeps fetialium, proficiscebatur ad hostium fines, et praefatus quadam sollemnia, clara voce dicebat se bellum indicere propter certas causas, aut quia socios laeserant aut quia nec abrepta animalia nec obnoxios redderent. et haec clarigatio dicebatur a claritate vocis. post quam clarigationem hasta in eorum fines missa indicabatur iam pugnae principium. post tertium autem et tricesimum diem quam res repetissent ab hostibus, fetiales hastam mittebant. denique cum Pyrrhi temporibus adversum transmarinum hostem bellum Romani gesturi essent nec invenirent locum, ubi hanc sollemnitatem per fetiales indicendi belli celebrarent, dederunt operam, ut unus de Pyrrhi militibus caperetur, quem fecerunt in circo Flaminio locum emere, ut **quasi in hostili loco** ius belli indicendi implerent. (Servius *ad Aen.* 9.52)[27]

BEGINNING OF BATTLE: this is what one needs to know concerning the Roman rite. When they wanted to declare war, the *pater patratus*, that is, the chief of the fetials, would set out for the enemy's border. There he would speak certain solemn pronouncements, saying in a clear voice that the Romans were declaring war for specific reasons, or because they had harmed allies of Rome, or because they had not returned animals they had stolen or captives they had seized. This is called the *clarigatio*, from the *claritas* of his voice. After the *clarigatio*, a spear is hurled into the enemy's territory, to indicate the commencement of hostilities. The fetials throw the spear at any time after the thirty-third day from the one on which they demanded restitution. Finally, when in the time of Pyrrhus the Romans were about to wage war against a *transmarinum hostem*, an enemy across the sea and could not find a place where they might perform through the fetials this ritual for declaring war, they compelled one of Pyrrhus' soldiers, a captive, to buy a plot of land near the *circus Flaminius*, so that they might fulfill the law of declaring war *quasi in hostili loco*, **as if** in hostile territory.

Both these cases describe revisions to ritual forms as the institutions of the classical city-state were (literally) stretched to the breaking point by the material conditions created by Roman imperial action. In the first passage, Gellius describes a change in the legal ritual for vindication of ownership "after the boundaries of Italy were extended," and it became impractical for the praetor to witness physical contact between a declarant and the property he claimed. In the second, Servius, the fourth-century commentator on Vergil, relying ultimately on the first-century BCE polymath Varro, describes a revision to the ritual of the fetial priests when Rome began to fight wars "against enemies across the sea," and it became impractical to declare war by hurling a symbolic spear into the enemy's territory and so ritually enacting the start of violence. The apparent violation of some earlier commitment to materiality underlying the ritual act is observed in the form of the aside that the change in the first case occurs *contra duodecim tabulas*, "contrary to the Twelve Tables." At the same time, in both cases, the change is understood to have been effected through a fiction, and hence the violation of principle might be said to be apparent, not real: vindication is made on a piece of the property in question **as if** on the whole; the spear is now hurled onto a plot of land that only notionally belongs to the enemy; the rite is therefore conducted "**as if** in hostile territory."

I conclude my remarks on religion with a reading of Varro's *Antiquitates rerum divinarum*.[28] As with the contrast drawn by Roman lawyers between natural law and the law of any given society, so in respect to religion Varro contrasted the institutions of "civic" religion with the speculations of philosophical theology. "Civic" religion is a human institution, built according to human epistemic capacities, to be judged solely in light of the norms of the society whose social order it secures.[29] The nature and power of that claim is rendered most clearly visible by judging it against two trends in his text: first, Varro clearly contrasts the principle of correctness in cult against truth claims in other epistemic domains; and second, he describes cult at Rome as the product of historical developments in which the sole agents are human.

In fragment 12, for example, Varro contrasts the potential to establish a religion on the basis of "nature" (*ex naturae formula*) with cult *in vetere populo*, in an ancient people:

> non se illa iudicio suo sequi, quae civitatem Romanam instituisse ... si eam civitatem novam constitueret, ex naturae potius formula deos nominaque eorum se fuisse dedicaturum. ... Sed iam quoniam in vetere populo esset, acceptam ab antiquis nominum et cognominum historiam tenere, ut tradita est, debere se ... et ad eum finem illa scribere et perscrutari, ut potius eos magis colere quam despicere vulgus velit. (Varro *Antiquitates rerum divinarum* fr. 12 Cardauns)

For [he confessed] that he did not pursue in accord with his own judgment the things that the Roman community had *institutuisse*, had established ... If he had been founding a new community, he would instead have consecrated the gods and their names according to the rule of nature. ... But as it was, as he was among an ancient people, he was obliged to hold to the history received from antiquity of names and *cognomina* as it was handed down ... and to record and examine them with this end in mind, that the common people should want to worship much more than to despise them.

In the civic religion of an ancient people, names, words, and formulae, however arbitrary, are among the things received from antiquity, and Varro understands his obligation to be precisely *not* to scrutizine the truth content of that *historia* but rather to ensure its efficacy in sustaining social order.

Elsewhere, Varro distinguished between his project in respect to religion as social practice from some abstract theological inquiry into the nature of the gods *per se* as follows:

propterea se prius de rebus humanis, de divinis autem postea scripsiss ..., quod prius extiterint civitates, deinde ab eis haec instituta sint. ... Sicut prior est ... pictor quam tabula picta, prior faber quam aedificium, ita priores sunt civitates quam ea, quae a civitatibus instituta sunt.

Si de omni natura deorum et hominum scriberemus, prius divina absolvissemus, quam humana adtigissemus. ... Rerum ... humanarum libros non quantum ad orbem terrarum, sed quantum ad solam Romam pertinet. (Varro *Antiquitates rerum divinarum* fr. 5 Cardauns)

Wherefore [Varro says that] he wrote first about human things and later about divine ones, because political communities come into being first and later the things instituted by them. Just as the painter is prior to the painting, or the builder to the building, so political communities are prior to those things that are instituted by political communities.

If I were writing about the totality of the nature of gods and humans, I should have completed the divine matters before I touched upon human matters. But the scope of the books on human affairs do not relate to the entire world, but to Rome alone.

Varro's claim at this juncture famously aroused the ire of Augustine, and his anger may be simply explained. For Christians, it was simply axiomatic that God's ontological priority sanctioned the authority of his Scripture, and the myths contained therein provide aetiologies for Christian rites. Assuming for the sake of argument that Varro wrote under similar beliefs, Augustine construes the organization of Varro's work as surrendering ontological priority to humans. But Varro had drawn a contrast Augustine declined to credit, namely, that religious institutions are the product of imperfect human striving after knowledge, within specific cultural and linguistic contexts, and their efficacy rested not on divine sanction of their form, but divine consent to their legitimacy. Even as Cicero had distinguished inquiry into universal law from that into the laws instituted among a given people, so in the context of civic theology, Varro could insist that "divine things" as they pertain to any given city are nothing more and nothing less than things *ab eis instituta*, things instituted by those cities.

As regards historical development, Varro records changes of two kinds: changes in cult practice, most particularly the switch from aniconic worship to cult involving images and the incremental addition of cult obligations to further gods.[30] A tertium quid might be the imposition of public controls – which is to say, the subjection to purely human authorities – of the discretion even of magistrates to impose additional cult obligations on the public.[31]

I close by pointing out just how far Varro's commitment to this theoretical position extends. There is first the claim, advanced in respect to the god Summanus, that his popularity rested not upon his power or immanence in itself, but upon the material presence of his cult in the city:

> Romani veteres ... Summanum, cui nocturna fulmina tribuebant, coluerunt magis quam Iovem, ad quem diurna fulmina pertinerent. Sed postquam Iovi templum insigne et sublime constructum est, propter aedis dignitatem sic ad eum multitudo confluxit, ut vix inveniatur qui Summani nomen, quod audire iam non potest, se saltem legisse meminerit. (Varro *Antiquitates rerum divinarum* fr. 42)

The ancient Romans worshipped Summanus, to whom they attributed nocturnal lightning, more than Jupiter, to whom daytime lightning pertained. But after an outstanding and lofty temple was built for Jupiter, a multitude turned to him because of the dignity of the building, with the result that scarcely anyone can be found who remembers having read the name of Summanus, which can now no longer be heard.

But Varro went further still. In the case of Summanus, it is merely his name that appears to have been effaced from contemporary memory and contemporary practice. But through their consensual construction of religion, humans also determined the fate of the gods themselves:

se timere ne pereant (sc. dei) non incursu hostili, sed civium neglegentia, de qua illos velut ruina liberari a se (dicit) et in memoria bonorum per eius modi libros recondi atque servari utiliore cura, quam Metellus de incendio sacra Vestalia et Aeneas de Troiano excidio penates liberasse praedicatur. (Varro *Antiquitates rerum divinarum* fr. 2A)

Varro said that he feared lest the gods should perish not from an enemy attack but the neglect of citizens, from which they were saved by him as if from a collapsing building and they were stored away and saved in the memory of the good through books of the sort he himself wrote. This was, he suggested, a more useful act than Metellus's having saved the relics of Vesta from fire or Aeneas's having saved the *penates* at the fall of Troy.

The negligence of the citizens would not cause the gods to depart, or turn their backs, as Apollo had at Tyre during the siege of Alexander. They would die, even as they might be saved by prodigious acts of historical memory.

6. My final example turns away from law and religion to cultural history. It concerns the construction of time as a social fact. I choose this example because, as with law and religion, so time could easily be regarded as having an ontology distinct from the social, as some sort of natural universal – as indeed it was. But that is not where Roman thought on time ended, as Pliny the Elder's study of time-keeping at Rome makes clear. Pliny turns to time-keeping in that section of the *Natural History* devoted to tacit social conventions. There he traces the history of time-keeping at Rome from the mid-fifth down to the mid-second century BCE (Pliny *Nat.*7.212–15, trans. Rackham):

(212) Tertius consensus fuit in horarum observatione, iam hic ratione accedens, quando et a quo in Graecia reperta, diximus secundo volumine. serius etiam hic Romae contigit. XII tabulis ortus tantum et occasus nominantur, post aliquot annos adiectus est et meridies, accenso consulum id pronuntiante, cum a curia inter Rostra et Graecostasin prospexisset solem; a columna Maenia ad carcerem inclinato sidere supremam pronuntiavit, sed hoc serenis tantum diebus, usque ad primum Punicum bellum.

The third (silent) agreement (among the nations) was in the observation of the hours < ... >, the date and inventor of which we have stated in book 2. This also happened later at Rome: in the Twelve Tables, only sunrise and sunset are specified; a few years later, noon was also added, the consuls' *apparitor* announcing it when from the *curia* he saw the sun between the *Rostra* and the Greek Guest House. When the sun sloped from the Maenian column to the prison he announced the last hour, but this only on clear days, down to the First Punic War.

(213) princeps solarium horologium statuisse ante undecim annos quam cum Pyrro bellatum est ad aedem Quirini L. Papirius Cursor, cum eam dedicaret a patre suo votam, a Fabio Vestale proditur. sed neque facti horologii rationem vel artificem significat nec unde translatum sit aut apud quem scriptum id invenerit.

We have it on the authority of Fabius Vestalis that the first sundial was erected eleven years before the war with Pyrrhus at the Temple of Quirinus by Lucius Papirius Cursor when dedicating that temple, which had been vowed by his father, but Fabius does not indicate the principle of the sundial's construction or its maker, nor where it was brought from or the writer who is his authority for the statement.

(214) M. Varro primum statutum in publico secundum Rostra in columna tradit bello Punico primo a M'. Valerio Messala cos. Catina capta in Sicilia, deportatum inde post XXX annos quam de Papiriano horologio traditur, anno urbis CCCCLXXXX. nec congruebant ad horas eius lineae, paruerunt tamen ei annis undecentum, donec Q. Marcius Philippus, qui cum L. Paulo fuit censor, diligentius ordinatum iuxta posuit, idque munus inter censoria opera gratissima acceptum est.

Marcus Varro records that the first public sundial was set up on a column along by the *rostra* during the First Punic War after Catania in Sicily had been taken by the consul Manius Valerius Messala, and that it was brought from Sicily thirty years later than the traditional date of Papirius' sundial, in the 490th year of the city. The lines of this sundial did not agree with the hours, but all the same they followed it for 99 years, until Quintus Marcius Philippus, who was censor with Lucius Paulus, placed a more carefully designed one next to it, and this gift was received as one of the most welcome of the censor's undertakings.

(215) etiam tum tamen nubilo incertae fuere horae usque ad proximum lustrum. tunc Scipio Nasica collega Laenati primus aqua divisit horas aeque noctium ac dierum idque horologium sub tecto dicavit anno urbis DXCV. tam diu populo Romano indiscreta lux fuit.

Even then, however, the hours were uncertain in cloudy weather, until the next *lustrum*, when Scipio Nasica the colleague of Laenas set up the first water clock dividing the hours of the nights and days equally, and dedicated this time piece in a roofed building in the 595th year of the city. For so long a period had the divisions of daylight not been marked for the Roman people.

For the early period Pliny relies on inferences from textual sources not directly concerned with time-keeping: the Twelve Tables, he observes, mentioned only two times of day, sunrise and sunset (§212). The later observation of noon, as also of the last hour before sunset, depended on the contingent material conditions of the urban landscape: an official observed the sun in relation to pre-determined features of the city-scape. (We are reminded of the role assigned by Varro to contingent aspects of the built environment in determining the popularity of gods.)

Rome later acquired sundials (§213–14), though some controversy attends the question when the first was acquired, and from whom. Notably, the sundial that Pliny credits as first was, by virtue of some fault, consistently wrong, even as mere human convention rendered its information dispositive and hence, after some fashion, correct: "The lines of this sundial did not agree with the hours, but all the same they followed it for 99 years."

What is more, the whole system to that date depended on the sky being clear: Rome achieved the ability to mark the hours in cloudy weather only in the 595th year of the city (159 BCE).

Time as social fact – social reality in its totality – is on this view created through the epistemic and political work of the community. It does not rest upon transcendent or natural norms. What is more, social reality at any given moment rests upon a consensus not simply about norms (how many hours shall there be and what shall be their length) but about the means for deriving and authorizing norms (what sort of clock shall we use, and who has the right to install it, and where).

7. I have focused thus far on Roman thought in respect to Roman institutions. I would like to close by returning to the issues with which I opened, and to the Roman insistence that the institutions of all other cities should be likewise understood. The implications of the language used by Gaius ("civil law is the law that each political community makes for itself") receives further elaboration in the *Institutes* of Justinian, who adopts the phrasing of the earlier textbook and illustrates with an example:

> Sed ius quidem civile ex unaquaque civitate appellatur, veluti Atheniensium: nam si quis velit Solonis vel Draconis leges appellare ius civile Atheniensium, non erraverit. sic enim et ius quo populus Romanus utitur ius civile Romanorum appellamus, vel ius Quiritium, quo Quirites utuntur; Romani enim a Quirino Quirites appellantur. sed quotiens non addimus, cuius sit civitatis, nostrum ius significamus: sicuti cum poetam dicimus nec addimus nomen, subauditur apud Graecos egregius Homerus, apud nos Vergilius. (Justinian *Inst.* 1.2.2)

A particular *ius civile* is named after an individual state, for example, the Athenians: for if someone wished to call the laws of Solon or Draco the *ius civile* of the Athenians, he would not err. So, too, we name the *ius civile* of the Romans that *ius* that the Roman populace uses, or the *ius Quiritium* that *ius* that the Quirites use, for the Romans are called Quirites from Quirinus. But when we add no word signifying the state whose law we discuss, we speak of our own *ius*; just as when we say "the poet" and add no name, among Greeks it is assumed that the excellent Homer is being named, but among us, Vergil.

Sed naturalia quidem iura, quae apud omnes gentes peraeque servantur, divina quadam providentia constituta, semper firma atque immutabilia permanent: ea vero quae ipsa sibi quaeque civitas constituit, saepe mutari solent vel tacito consensu populi vel alia postea lege lata. (Justinian *Inst.* 1.2.11)

But natural laws, which are observed uniformly among all peoples, are established by a certain divine providence, and abide fixed and immutable; the laws that each community establishes for itself, on the other hand, are accustomed to be changed often, either by the tacit consent of the people or by the passage of a new statute.

Within such an understanding, law can be understood historically only by reference to the community that produces its contingent articulation, and must first be assessed in relation to the social order it is called upon to secure. The same is true at the level of language: laws are products of linguistic communities, too, and they can only succeed as long as it is agreed that their language successfully describes the worlds they are called upon to regulate.

Likewise regarding religion: the historical relativism and epistemic humility expressed by Varro – which was shared by Cicero and Pliny, and Livy and Trajan and Gaius – worked to support a distinctively imperial mode of religious tolerance, in which the constituent communities of the empire (which is to say, those recognized *as* communities *by* the empire), were permitted and, indeed, encouraged to maintain their pre-existing religious practices.[32] For where Augustine invoked a faith directed at an avowedly a priori body of doctrine, credited with a source and status transcendent to the knowledge systems of any given culture, the gaps and slippages created by Roman sceptical argument direct attention instead to the contribution any given religion makes to the flourishing of its community.

It is of course not possible now to say whether this understanding of the ontology of the social pre-existed Rome's expansion beyond the confines of central Italy. There may have been a time when Romans' contact with peoples recognized as other to themselves was nonetheless limited to those with largely homologous institutions; and relations with such people will have required no background understanding to sustain cognition or recognition in respect to cultural difference.[33] But the moment came when the pursuit of empire required such an understanding, and the one visible in Roman texts is distinctive in comparison with other such understandings visible in the texts of other ancient cultures. What is more, it harmonized closely, and thus collaborated, with the commitment to contractualism and the quite limited conception of political identity that we studied in chapters 1 and 2, to sustain a polity of remarkable heterogeneity.

CONCLUSION

Making Romans

1. Allow me in closing to reflect on some historical problems whose contours may be clarified in light of the arguments thus far advanced, and at the same time to extend consideration to additional figures contiguous to those I have considered.

2. I have several times urged that empires function through the cultivation of difference. Salient axes of difference might be drawn between metropolitan and subaltern populations, as between subaltern populations themselves. In the Roman case, this was done in part through regulatory mechanisms that sought to control geographic aspects of social and economic conduct, in order to rive colonized populations, one from another, and prevent the realization of solidarity between them. Instead, each of them was bound through purely bilateral relations to the metropole. This work was also performed through the juridical classification of persons and populations, who, whatever they were before (and remained), were now also classed and sorted in the superordinate schema of empire, as citizens, Latins, and aliens.

A common entailment of empires so organized is the notional equality before the law of all persons holding metropolitan citizenship, such that those belonging to the centre are equal among themselves in contradistinction to those over whom they as a collective rule. In empires otherwise organized, there exists a single or unified logic of social differentiation, which extends uniformly through the population and establishes metropolitans and others in mutual relation in a single hierarchical scheme. In these latter political formations, the salience of various forms of cultural difference is likely to be rather different than in the former.[1]

These are, of course, ideal types: their realization in any given empire, and the durability of that form, will vary according to cultural factors that are themselves subject to historical change. What is more, the viability of any given schema must surely depend in part upon the scale of interaction among populations, itself a function of cultural, material, and ecological factors, so that one or another form is more common in sea-, steppe-, or land-based empires, and so on.

Rome constitutes a special case in many such taxonomies of empire because it passed from one type to another: from a political form in which citizenship functioned as a primary mechanism of social differentiation to one in which all free persons were deemed Romans, at which point other mechanisms had perforce to come to the fore.[2]

At no point in this long history does Rome produce a significant discourse on cultural difference: ethnography rarely focused its lens on peoples within the empire; for all their capaciousness, geographies *of* the empire read more as catalogues than reflections on self and other; differences in custom and law are treated by Roman authorities as problems of jurisdiction or particularities of international private law rather than crises of norms of moral, ethical, or political significance.[3] One might employ as an index or proxy of this lack the non-attestation in the classical period of any term like *Romanitas*, meaning "Romanness," formed from *Romanus* as *civitas* is from *civis*, abstracting and essentializing that quality or those features that all Romans share and that make them Roman.[4] How are we to explain this?

Chapter 1 argued that Romans understood political belonging principally on a contractualist model: it was voluntary assent to the normative strictures of the community and collaboration in matters of shared utility that made one Roman. Inter alia, I pointed there to the role played by voluntary associations and private contract relations in the source domain of explanatory moves in respect to political collectivities. Let me attempt to affirm and extend that argument by considering two further expressions, *fundus fieri* and *Romani facti*. The former phrase means something like, "to become landed or part of the soil," or perhaps, "to take root"; the latter, "to become Roman." I take them in turn.

I so bracket my own translation of *fundus fieri* because, while the expression is clearly metaphorical, it is also obscure. The earliest attestations of the term *fundus* belong to two seemingly discrete contexts: it can refer to a farm, and in particular to a farm established on soil granted by, or rented from, the Roman people; and it can refer to persons who serve as guarantors of particular social or legal relations – who are, as it were, their foundation or base.[5] The tight metaphorical connection between affective and normative commitment, on the one hand, and land and soil on the other, is something we have already had occasion to explore, and *fundus* obviously constitutes another nodal point in that complex.

Regarding the phrase *fundus fieri*, which occurs exclusively in public-law contexts, there exists very general agreement about what it means, though some disagreement at the margins about the technicalities of the situations to which it is applied.[6] My interest lies solely in its status as figurative and the ascription of agency it performs. The earliest use of, and most extended reflection on, the figure occurs in Cicero's *pro Balbo*, when Cicero considers situations in which an alien community chooses to adopt a particular piece of Roman legislation as normative over itself:

> Quid enim potuit dici imperitius quam foederatos populos fieri fundos oportere? nam id non magis est proprium foederatorum quam omnium liberorum. Sed totum hoc, iudices, in ea fuit positum semper ratione atque sententia ut, cum iussisset populus Romanus aliquid, si id adscivissent socii populi ac Latini, et si ea lex, quam nos haberemus, eadem in populo aliquo tamquam in fundo resedisset, ut tum lege eadem is populus teneretur, non ut de nostro iure aliquid deminueretur, sed ut illi populi aut iure eo quod a nobis esset constitutum aut aliquo commodo aut beneficio uterentur. (Cicero *pro Balbo* 20)

What could be said with greater ignorance than that allied peoples ought to become *fundus*? This condition no more belongs to allies than it does to free peoples. In fact, jurymen, this whole practice was always based upon this principle and intention, that, when the Roman people ordered something (i.e., made a law), if allied peoples and the Latins adopted it, and if the very same law that we observe had, as it were, settled down in some citizen body *tamquam in fundo*, **as it were in the soil**, then that people would be bound by the same law not in such a way that anything is diminished in respect to our law, but in such a way that those communities might make use of the law established by us or of some other advantage or benefit.

Postremo haec vis est istius et iuris et verbi, ut fundi populi beneficio nostro, non suo iure fiant. Cum aliquid populus Romanus iussit, id si est eius modi ut quibusdam populis, sive foederatis sive liberis, permittendum esse videatur ut statuant ipsi non de nostris sed de suis rebus, quo iure uti velint, tum utrum fundi facti sint an non quaerendum esse videatur; de nostra vero re publica, de nostro imperio, de nostris bellis, de victoria, de salute fundos populos fieri noluerunt. (Cicero *Balb.* 21–2)

In sum, the substance of that principle of law and of its language is this, that peoples become *fundus* not of their own legal right but by our favour. When the Roman people has ordered something, if it is of such a kind that it seems appropriate to allow certain communities, whether allied or free, to decide for themselves, by reference not to our but to their own affairs, what law they wish to use, then it seems appropriate to ask whether or not those peoples have become *fundus* [i.e., as a factual matter, in a particular legal deliberation]. But when the matter concerns our *res publica*, our empire, our wars, our victory, our safety: then our ancestors did not want those peoples to become *fundus*.

In the first passage, Cicero uses the term *fundus* both of the people who establish a law as normative over themselves and of the law itself; on one occasion, when speaking of a law becoming *fundus*, he also flags the term as metaphorical (via *tamquam*), very likely because an inanimate abstraction like a law does not possess the agency that the import of the phrase seeks to capture. That becoming *fundus* is voluntary, which is to say, that taking a law unto oneself and assenting both to its content and the legitimacy of its mode of production are understood normatively as matters of consent, is revealed in the second passage, where Cicero reassures his Roman audience that it always lay within its power to impose law in matters of its interest, in which case the issue of consent, of a people's becoming *fundus*, was irrelevant.

The phrase *Romanos fieri*, "to become Roman," likewise appears to be a term of art in Roman public law, being used already in this form by Ennius.[7] It is clearly not metaphorical. It reveals, rather, the importance as well as the limits of consent to law in Roman conceptions of political belonging. Consider, for example, a moment early in Livy's narrative when different outcomes are imagined for discrepant participants to Rome's war with the Hernici. At the conclusion of that conflict, Roman citizenship was imposed on all defeated parties. To three constituent communities who had sided with Rome in the war, however, citizenship was merely offered: they preferred that their laws and rights of intermarriage should be returned, an ancient shorthand for retaining their status as autonomous polities.[8] Not long thereafter, their example was cited by the Aequi, whom the Romans had threatened with war:

> ... temptationem aiebant esse ut terrore incusso belli Romanos se fieri paterentur; quod quanto opere optandum foret, Hernicos docuisse, cum quibus licuerit suas leges Romanae ciuitati praeoptauerint; quibus legendi quid mallent copia non fuerit, pro poena necessariam ciuitatem fore. (Livy 9.45.6–8)

> [The Aequi] responded that the Roman approach was merely an attempt to force them, under threat of war, to suffer themselves to become Romans. The Hernici had shown how greatly this was to be desired, when it was granted to them to choose and they had preferred their own laws to Roman citizenship. To those to whom the opportunity of choosing was not given, citizenship would necessarily be *pro poena*, a form of punishment.

It is clear that "to become Roman" was normatively conceived as a voluntary act, though obviously it is the falseness of the choice that the Aequi in Livy's representation seek to expose. Importantly, however, similar language can be used of Romans resigning their citizenship to enrol in a Latin colony. The term "Latin colony" refers to colonial foundations in which the population had the legal status of Latins, and Romans who enrolled in those colonies could be described as having "become Latin."[9] The phrases *Romanos fieri* and *Romani facti* – like *fundus fieri* – should therefore be understood as grammatical middles, kindred to the classical terms *hellênizô* and its cognates (*hellênizesthai, hellênismos*), which only start to be used transitively, with the meaning "to [forcibly] make Greek," in the Hellenistic period in the context of empire. Like *fundus fieri*, however, which, as we have seen, was simply not applied when law was imposed, the transitive form, *Romanos facere*, "to [forcibly] make someone Roman," does not occur.

Another feature of the term's usage is also worth noting: one becomes Roman by becoming juridically Roman. Nowhere in any classical Roman text that I can think of does one make oneself Roman – self-fashion as Roman in language or dress or cuisine – in order to appear worthy of citizenship. Of course, in practice something like this no doubt occurred, but crucially, in the Roman imagination cultural change and juridical belonging were susceptible of radical decoupling. Occasionally people confused about their own legal status are described as conducting themselves as Romans – wearing togas, using Roman nomenclature in its full, formal sense, serving on juries, marrying Romans, and writing Roman wills – but the language used in such cases is nearly always *pro cive gerere*, to conduct oneself as/as if a citizen.[10] Citizenship, *civitas*, is what all Romans shared, and apparently it successfully captured all that they shared.[11]

3. The aftermath of the war with the Hernici is a salutary reminder that Roman citizenship, which is to say, republican citizenship, was not always a reward or badge of membership, a talisman of legal rights and privileges. On the contrary, citizenship appears to have been one of two primary means for the extension of state power, the other being the confiscation of alien land as *ager publicus*, property of the Roman state. In the early Roman state, if something – a body, a field – was not Roman, it was not governed.

In regard to the early history of Rome, we are of course nearly wholly at the mercy of sources of a much later period, and so we cannot say anything with certainty about the languages of contemporary politics and therefore little of precision in respect to ideologies of empire and political belonging. But it was, I suspect, the use of (defective forms of) citizenship to embrace conquered populations that promoted the development within Roman culture of distinctive forms of tolerance and tolerance for diversity – or the causal chain may have worked the other way around. In any event, though, being Romans, their official memory retained and transmitted a record of these early forcible impositions of citizenship, they also came to tell a quite different story about the originary moment of their community, to wit, the myth of Romulus's asylum. Whatever else it does, that myth provides a potent explanatory gloss on the internal heterogeneity of the Roman community.[12]

The internal heterogeneity of the Roman community that was the product of empire – and the means by which empire brought people to Rome were of course numerous – in turn provoked the creation and consolidation of another linguistic-institutional apparatus for sustaining it, namely, the public–private distinction. The lexical complex *privo/privatus* refers, of course, to an act of deprivation or withdrawal: that which is private is something from which the community has withdrawn its claim.[13] I put the matter thus to distinguish Roman thought in respect to the private, and especially private property, from ideologies of private property in the liberal tradition. For participants in the latter, private property has an ontology prior to the state and, indeed, the state can be described as having its raison d'être in the (mutual) protection of private property claims. But in Roman republican ideology, all was public until the state withdrew its claim: as the myth of asylum among other evidence affirms, individuals arrive in the Roman state shorn of all property. Indeed, in contrast also to the Greek tradition, in Roman thought not even the household or family has an ontology that antedates the city. As we saw in chapter 3, history itself commences *ab urbis initiis*.

To appreciate the work performed by the public–private distinction in regulating, explaining, and bracketing the internal heterogeneity of the imperial republic, consider the second law offered by Cicero in the draft constitution contained in his work *On the Laws*, which urges as follows:

Separatim nemo habessit deos, neve novos neve advenus, nisi **publice** adscitos.

Privatim colunto quos rite a patribus <cultos acceperint.> (Cicero *Leg.* 2.19)

Let no one have gods separately, either new or foreign, unless they have been recognized publicly.

Let them worship in private those whose worship has been duly handed down by their ancestors.

Latent in these clauses are potential ruptures at several levels. First, it seems clear from the distinction Cicero draws between "having a god separately (*separatim*)" and "having a god privately (*privatim*)" that he distinguishes actions by two kinds of individuals: those holding magistracies, and hence holding the power potentially to bind the community, and those in private station. It is precisely the power of magistrates to affect state cult that he seeks to foreclose. This had for some time been a concern in Roman public life, as Varro, too, attests, and legislation had long since sought to deal with it.[14] (For historians of religion, these clauses raise the question of how public recognition of a deity was understood to obligate or affect individuals in their private practices or, to the matter the other way around, how the commitment of individual citizens to civic cult was conceived. That is not a matter I can take up here.)[15] Conversely, the Roman community regularly acquired new citizens, and such immigrants would come with gods. For them, that which was duly handed down would for others be foreign and new. Setting aside the niceties of its operation, one can see how a public–private distinction so conceived might serve as a firewall between notionally separate spheres of religious obligation, one communal, the other familial, preserving the public or statal as shared and bracketing the private as of no concern outside those who conceive any given commitment as binding.[16] The diversity of private cult thus existed for the state purely as a theoretical problem and its existence was recognized only in that ideated form; its actualities being deemed beyond state interest, the diversity of cult among the newly enfranchised persisted outside elite knowledge interests altogether.

By the year 300 BCE or so, Rome ceased to impose citizenship on the conquered and came instead to employ various forms of juridical distinction between Romans and others as a structural principle of its empire as a political form. This transformation helped to endow the political community with a new ontology, which enabled new narratives of its history and new arguments in social theory to the come to the fore. Part and parcel of this transformation was the coming to prominence of doctrines of citizenly equality and popular sovereignty, which are in various forms visible already in the third century (in respect to equality before the law) and the later second (in regard to popular sovereignty).[17] The myth of asylum, the public–private distinction, and contractualist models of states as voluntary associations all find their place in this long history.

This transformation in Roman self-understanding in regard to the historical ontology of political communites had profound implications for how they understood the particularities of social and cultural life in territories that they ruled but whose residents were now deemed alien. The genesis, scope, and strength of Roman toleration in its imperial mode should be attributed to this developmental process, whereby an imperial state that had once forcibly (and, for practical reasons, likely only minimally) assimilated foreigners as citizens gradually committed to a new practice of juridical distinction at the level of empire and a new ideology of juridical equality at the level of the state. In this new dispensation, the internal heterogeneity of the imperial republic required normative explanation. When applied to other polities, especially those subordinated to Rome, the social–theoretical apparatus thus called into being gave rise to an epistemic and moral relativism of extraordinary richness.

As a related matter, the Roman example urges two further considerations. First, at Rome an imperial mode of toleration existed alongside a civil one. Though the two are capable of disarticulation for purposes of analysis and comparison, their historical conjuncture rested in the Roman case on dialectical developments in the ideology and practice of imperial politics. The point deserves comparative historical study. Second, the subsequent era of assimilation of aliens to Romans, which is to say, the extension of a monarchic republican citizenship ultimately to all free-born residents of the empire, should be studied in light of the normative apparatus here outlined. The highly abstract homologies that I have discerned in Roman toleration in its classical guises, both imperial and civil, served to sustain substantial political, social, and material realities of difference at the level of practice, which in turn became the crucible in which the new post-Antonine state was forged.

4. Many of the topics that I have discussed – the distinction between the legal, the natural, and the social; the material basis of affective attachment; the percipience and ontology of social realities – exist in tight correlation with problematics in historical epistemology. I conclude, therefore, with some reflections on Roman knowledge.

There is a minor but non-trivial literature in modern security studies that takes as its point of departure the apparent coining of the word *certitudo*, certainty, in Christian late antiquity – it is first securely attested in Gregory the Great – and posits the birth at that moment of particular conceptions of security, certainty, and risk.[18] At some level, that entire project rests on a set of methodological fallacies: there is no reason to believe Gregory was the first to coin the word, nor any reason to focus on *certitudo* over against the enormous importance of *certus* and *certiorem facere* in classical Latin. This is not to say, however, that certainty has no history, nor that the triumph of Platonizing metaphysics through the vehicle of Christianity, by which the fallible and transient here-and-now became dispreferred to a transcendent world beyond some eschaton, played no role in that history.

Certus is often translated "certain," and this is no doubt often adequate. In light of the concerns outlined in chapter 3, however, it bears recalling that *certus* is in fact a perfective passive participle, from *cerno*, which can in various contexts be translated "to see" or "to distinguish," and also "to resolve." In the last meaning it is used above all of legally binding decisions by parties to statally supervised procedings. *Cerno* thus participates in much the same field as its relative, *decerno*, which can likewise mean to decide, to determine, to resolve, and also to decree. What is "certain" is therefore things of two kinds: those that have been empirically verified, by sense perception and above all by sight; and those that have been affirmed. (The metaphorical status of acts of mental discernment is perhaps acknowledged in the frequent specification that such acts take place *oculis animi*, with the eyes of the mind, and so forth.) Put the other way around, it is acts of judgment by social and statal authorities that create the preconditions for certainty and, therefore, likewise for knowledge.

A similar claim could be made in respect to *scisco*, to ascertain, to seek to know, but also to approve, decree, ordain, whose perfective passive participle forms the basis of *plebiscitum*, plebiscite. We observe in its range in the classical period a similarly tight nexus between that which is knowable and that which has been socially and authoritatively affirmed: of course, as Cicero says, one enacts legislation *re cognita*, once the facts are known, but the binding decision of a sovereign body both ratifies that act of knowing and itself creates new social facts, which are binding within, and knowable by, the community that endows that body with sovereign power.[19]

5. To govern the world that their political and imperial action had created, indeed, to bring that world into being, the Romans had to be able to grasp it in its totality, in all its myriad particularities and also its essentials. The distinctions they drew between those two categories; the means they devised to bracket particularities as of narrowly local concern; the abstraction of categories by which those particularities might be classified, compared, and understood; and the way those taxonomic operations allowed issues of cultural and ecological difference to emerge to salience or regress into background: all these acts of understanding were realized in a language that took shape in relation to the needs it was asked to meet and the world it was called upon to describe. Cognition was thus a precondition of empire as practice, and the extraordinary figuration of classical Latin was its product.

Notes

Introduction

1 This seems an appropriate moment to acknowledge the enormous benefit that I have derived from Max Black's *Models and Metaphor*, esp. 25–47 and 220–43, which I first encountered in J.Z. Smith's magical *Drudgery Divine*, esp. 36–53.
2 Taylor, *Modern Social Imaginaries*. For a rich consideration of Taylor's volume within contemporary social theory, not least in light of his own earlier work, see Abbey, "Back to Baczko."
3 There is thus also a degree of affinity between my concern for the relationship between social imaginary and structures of language and that of Cornelius Castoriadis, with his concern for the relationship between social imaginary and the symbolic (Castoriadis, *The Imaginary Institution of Society*).
4 Foucault, *The Order of Things*; Pocock, *The Machiavellian Moment*.
5 Certainly the most brilliant effort known to me is Claudia Moatti's beautiful work, *La raison de Rome*.
6 Béranger, *Aspect idéologique*; idem, *Principatus*; Richardson, *The Language of Empire*; Lavan, *Slaves to Rome*.
7 In this sense, a more direct antecedent to this work might be the singular study of Larue van Hook, *Metaphorical Terminology*. For a related and suggestive use of grammar in the study of figure, at the dawn of cognitive studies of metaphor, see Christine Brooke-Rose, *A Grammar of Metaphor*.

1 Belonging

1 Vico, *The New Science*, p. 358 §971. The original runs: *Miserevolmente oppressi furon i cartaginesi, i quali dal Romano avevano*

ricevuta la pace sotto la legge che sarebbero loro salve la vita, la città e le sostanze, intentendo essi la «città» per gli «edifici», che da' latini si dice «urbs». Ma, perchè dal Romano si era usata la voce «civitas», che significa «comune di cittadini» ... (Vico, *La Scienza Nuova*, 465).

2 On interanimation see Turner, "Figure," 44–51; see also Lakoff and Turner, *More than Cool Reason*, 45–55.

3 On these passages and the relationship between Roman rules of jurisdistion and Roman theories of legal pluralism see Ando, "Law and the Landscape of Empire"; idem, *Law, Language and Empire*, 1–18; and Kantor, "*Siculus cum Siculo*."

4 That said, we should not be mislead by Cicero's language into thinking that the laws of these separate communities were utterly or even substantially different: they undoubtedly varied on certain features and particulars, while still sharing significant aspects of content, process, and structure. That is to say, Cicero's language (and perhaps my own) might lead one to imagine a situation of atomized particularity, rather than a continuum within which there are all sorts of Wittgensteinian family resemblances.

5 On this point see also Ando, *Religion et Gouvernement*, chapter 3; an earlier version of this text is available in a translation by Gian Franco Chiai, Ralph Häussler and Christiane Kunst, "Die Riten der Anderen"; see also idem, "The Edict of Serdica."

6 For further elaboration on these points see Ando, "Law and the Landscape of Empire," and idem, "The Roman City in the Roman Period."

7 Pliny *Nat.* 5.29–30.

8 Pliny *Nat.* 3.135, 138: Pliny draws on an Augustan list of peoples conquered under that emperor and then remarks, "Not included here are 15 *Cottianae civitates* which had not been hostile, nor those that were subordinated to municipalities by the Pompeian law."

9 I have written a great deal on this topic in recent years, all of it indebted to Shaw, "Autonomy and Tribute."

10 On this understanding of empire see Ando, "Imperial Identities."

11 I expand on these claims, with specific reference to the history of political subjectivity, in *Religion et Gouvernement*, chapter 1. For a related study of residence and citizenship in the Roman law tradition see Cavallar and Kirshner, "Jews as Citizens."

12 Ando, "Cities, Citizenship." As John Weisweiler points out to me, this transformation has an important correlate in developments in the concept of residence under the empire. Normally, one had

residence in a single community, the one whence one's family sprang and to which one owed a variety of legal duties; in any other place, one was merely a visitor. An exception was made in the case of senators, who were required to maintain a residence in Italy, regardless where their families originated. In the words of the jurist Paul: "Although senators appear to have residence in the City [which is to say, in Rome], nevertheless they are also understood to have residence in the place whence they sprang, since their rank seems to have granted an additional right of residence rather than to have changed the one they had" (Paul *Ad Edictum* bk. 41 fr. 574 Lenel = *Dig.* 1.9.11). On the impact of empire on the structures of citizenship see Yan Thomas, *"Origine" et "commune patrie."*

13 On this text see Chastagnol, "La législation sur les biens des villes," and Lenski, *Failure of Empire*, 295–6.

14 On *postliminium* see *RE* 22.1 (1953) 863–73 s.v. *postliminium* (H. Kreller). For an attempt to exploit law on *postliminium* to access Roman notions of territoriality and sovereignty see Ando, "Aliens, Ambassadors."

15 Paul *Ad Sabinum* bk. 16 fr. 1893 Lenel = *Dig.* 49.15.19.*pr.*; see also idem *Ad Sabinum* bk. 16 fr. 1893 Lenel = *Dig.* 49.15.19.3. See also Livy 3.2.12, where the Aequi retreat after a defeat *in fines suos.*

16 Paul *apud* Festus s.v. *postliminium* 245L: *Postliminium receptus dicitur is, qui extra limina, hoc est terminos provinciae, captus fuerat, rursus ad propria revertitur.*

17 As an aside, I observe that the diction of Paul's "abbreviation" bears almost no relation to that employed by Festus.

18 Cicero *Cat.* 4.16.

19 Livy 5.49.3.

20 Livy 2.1.5.

21 Livy 5.30.1–3.

22 Livy 21.53.4.

23 Livy 5.54.2; see also Ovid *Met.* 7.52 and 8.184, *Fasti* 3.291–2; and Velleius 2.7.7, quoted below.

24 Livy 5.37.8.

25 Ando, *Law, Language*, 37–63.

26 Varro *Ling.* 5.33: *Ut nostri augures publici disserunt, agrorum sunt genera quinque: Romanus, Gabinus, peregrinus, hosticus, incertus.*

27 Varro *Calenus* [*Logistorici* fr. 2 Semi = Servius *ad Aen.* 9.52]: *Varro in Caleno ita ait duces cum primum hostilem agrum introituri erant, ominis causa prius hastam in eum agrum mittebant, ut castris locum caperent.*

28 Livy 7.40.6.
29 Pliny *Ep.* 10.49–50. I translate *capax* with "capacious" in order to highlight the metaphorical status of its usage to denominate capacity *to do*.
30 On this passage see Ando, "Diana on the Aventine."
31 To wit, via private as opposed to statal action.
32 On exile see now Stini, *Plenum exiliis mare*, 29–54.
33 It is important to emphasize the distinctiveness of the term *solum* in this political-legal discourse. The parallel phrase, *terram vertere*, for example, is merely a periphrasis for *arare*, "to plow" (see Servius *ad Georg.* 1.2: *terram vertere* περιπηραστικῶς *arare*). Relatively late in the classical period *terra* does come to designate a piece of land to which a thing or individual has special attachment, and one can then speak of transplanting a tree or moving an individual from place to place using the phrase *terram mutare* (noted by OLD s.v. *terra* 7D, a singularly unhelpful entry; a search of TLL s.v. *muto* suggests the phrase was never made to perform the social theoretical work of *solum vertere*).
34 On denaturalization see the splendid work of Patrick Weil on twentieth-century American law, *The Sovereign Citizen*.
35 In addition to passages cited below see, e.g., Livy 21.63.9 and 43.2.10.
36 Livy 3.13.8.
37 Livy 2.2.10–11.
38 Livy 5.43.44 at 44.1, where Livy writes as though he has forgotten the status of Ardea as a citizen colony (cf. 4.9-11).
39 Cicero *Quinct.* 86.
40 But cf. *Paradoxa Stoicorum* 31: "All criminal and impious individuals ... whom the law wishes to be punished with exile are exiles, even if they do not change soil" (*Omnes scelerati atque impii ... quos leges exilio affici volunt exules sunt etiam si solum non mutarunt*).
41 Cicero *pro Caecina* 98–100.
42 Ando, "Vergil's Italy."
43 The fundamental modern text is Taylor, *Voting Districts*.
44 The scope of this work does not permit me to treat all the historical problems involved in this issue, but let me say for now that the restriction of freed slaves to the four urban tribes regardless of place of residence is further evidence of their artifactual quality.
45 On territories with two tribes see Taylor, *Voting Districts*, 319–23.
46 See *TLL* s.v. and cf. Clifford Ando, "Was Rome a *Polis*?," 22.

47 See Ando, "Vergil's Italy," on Cicero, *Contra Rullum* 2.93–5.

48 Salvian *De gubernatione dei* 4.54 (*cur vinci a barbaris patitur? cur iuri hostium subiugari?*), 5.47 (*Miserti quippe exulum non sumus, ecce ipsi exules sumus: peregrinos fraude cepimus, ecce ipsi peregrinamur; praeiudiciis temporum ingenui status homines circumvenimus, ecce ipsi nuper quidem in alieno solo vivere coepimus, sed praeiudicia iam timemus*); see also 7.7: the barbarians are "masters of Roman soil" (*dominos soli ... Romani*).

49 Eugippus *Vita Sancti Severini* 31.6: *Ipse vero Favianis degens in antiquo suo monasterio nec admonore populos nec praedicere futura cessabat, asserens universos in romani soli provinciam absque ullo libertatis migraturos incommodo.*

2 Cognition

1 Vico, *Institutiones Oratoriae*, chapter 39, *De tropis*, 310: *Tropi sunt qui vocem a propria ac nativa significatione ad impropriam et alienam deflectunt... Eius mutationis duae videntur causae, necessitas et ornatus. Necessitas ea fuit, quod cum verba, ut inquit iurisconsultus, sint rerum notae, et multo plures sint in natura res verbis: hinc quaeque lingua in quamplurimis rebus proprio vocabulo destituitur, eoque aliena accersenda fuere.* Readers may also consult the fine English translation of this work by Pinton and Shippee, *Art of Rhetoric*. On the identity of the jurist who wrote about words and things, see below at n. 22.

2 On this theme see Ando, *Law, Language*, 19–36; idem, *Imperial Rome*, 76–99; idem, *Religion et Gouvernement*, chapter 3.

3 On imperial citizenship and the potential dangers to the self-understanding of the center see Ando, "Making Romans"; for consideration of the same problem in respect to immigration in modern national states see Taylor, "The Dynamics of Democratic Exclusion," and cf. Ando, "Three Revolutions."

4 For another example see Hyginus *De condicionibus agrorum* 88.23–32 Campbell.

5 Vitruvius 2.9.15–16: When Julius Caesar was passing through and ordered the town to supply his army, it did not comply. He ordered soldiers to pile wood against the palisade and burn it down. When he noticed that the palisade did not catch fire, he reconsidered: would the town trade with him for its fire-retardant wood? Although Roman authors name the town *Larignum*, "Larch," we do not know whether the wood was named after the town or, as seems possible,

the town was named by imperial authorities after the product that placed it on the map.

6 Breton, *Inscriptions forestières*.

7 Ulpian bk. 71 *ad edictum* fr. 1613 Lenel = *Dig*. 43.28.*pr*.–1., citing Lenel *Edictum* Tit. 43 §–260.

8 Ulpian *ad Sabinum* fr. 2867 Lenel = *Dig*. 19.5.14.

9 Ulpian *ad edictum* fr. 721 Lenel = *Dig*. 10.4.9.1.

10 In other words, there is *lignum* that is *lignum* and *lignum* that is not.

11 For an interesting attempt to analyse the relationship between synecdoche and metonymy see Nerlich and Clarke, "Synecdoche as a Cognitive and Communicative Strategy."

12 On analogy in Roman legal argument see Ando, "*Exemplum*, Analogy and Precedent," and idem, "Fact, Fiction."

13 Consider by way of example the sample formula in *Lex de Gallia Cisalpina* chapter 20 (*RS* no. 28), where the names Q. Licinius and L. Seius are employed as placeholders, to be replaced by the names of the actual parties to the dispute as needed.

14 Cf. Hermogenianus bk. 2 *Iuris Epitomarum* fr. 54 Lenel = *Dig*. 27.1.41.

15 Roman Jakobson famous contrasted the role of "positional role and semantic contiguity" in metonymy with the role of similarity and analogy in metaphor ("Two Aspects of Language and Two Types of Aphasic Disturbances," in Jakobson and Halle, *Fundamentals*, 55–82). I am not alone in being unsure exactly what distinction he draws and how he intends these terms to be understood; nevertheless, the essay has spawned a considerable literature and remains worth rereading for its sweep and suggestiveness.

16 Julian bk. 84 *Digest* fr. 819 Lenel = *Dig*. 1.3.32.*pr*.

17 Paul bk. 5 *ad Plautium* fr. 1117 Lenel = *Dig*. 19.4.2.

18 I was inspired to this inquiry by a fantastic workshop by Jean-Jacques Aubert, a paper now published as "For Swap or Sale?"

19 Paul bk. 33 *ad edictum* fr. 502 Lenel = *Dig*. 19.4.1.4 (where the excerpt is attributed to bk. 32). The other action commonly made available to bartering parties was the so-called *actio praescriptis verbis*, on which see Berger, *Encyclopedic Dictionary*, s.v.

20 *Codex Iustinianus* 4.64.1 (*ad exemplum*), from 238 CE; *Codex Iustinianus* 4.64.2 (*vicem emptionis*), from 294 CE.

21 *Codex Iustinianus* 4.64.4, from 294 CE; *Codex Iustinianus* 4.64.7, from 294 CE.

22 Ulpian *Ad Sabinum* bk. 30 fr. 2747 Lenel = *Dig*. 19.5.4: *Natura enim rerum conditum est, ut plura sint negotia quam vocabula*. On

the jurists and the need for interpretation, see Ando, *Law, Language*, 19–36; idem, "Fact, Fiction"; and idem, "*Exemplum*, Analogy."

23 On the Twelve Tables see Gellius *Noctes Atticae* 20.1, esp. 20.1.5–6, 22.

24 So-called expansion of the law is of course a topic that has inspired a massive bibliography. A particularly creative and inspiring work in this field, not least because of its explicit use of metaphor, is Clark, "The Morphogenesis of Subchapter C."

25 For a technical study of prorogation and further bibliography see Ando, "Republican Constitutionalism"; see also Richardson, "The Roman Mind," 119–23.

26 Livy 8.23.10–12; see also 10.22.9: *Consules creati Q. Fabius et P. Decius, Ap. Claudius praetor, omnes absentes; et L. Volumnio ex senatus consulto et scito plebis prorogatum in annum imperium est* ("Quintius Fabius and Publius Decius were created consuls, Appius Claudius was created praetor; all three were elected in absentia. To Lucius Volumnius, on the advice of the Senate and a decree of the plebs, *imperium* was granted without election for one year").

27 *Fasti triumphales capitolini* = A. Degrassi, ed., *Inscriptiones Italiae*, vol. 13, fasc. 1 (1947), 70–1, year 326 B.C.E. = A.U.C. 428, recording the first prorogation: *Q. Publilius Q. f. Q. n. Philo II ann. CDXXVII primus pro co(n)s(ule) de Samnitibus, Palaeopolitaneis k. Mai.*

28 Cf. Isidore *Etymologiae* 9.3.8, with the translation by Barney et al.: *Proconsules suffecti erant consulibus, et dicti proconsules eo quod vicem consulis fungerentur, sicut procurator curatori, id est actori* ("Proconsuls were substitutes for consuls, and were called proconsuls because they would function in the place of consuls, as a procurator does in the place of curator, that is, an agent").

29 Livy 38.42.8–10: "A rumor was growing stronger day by day that a great war brewing ever stronger among the Ligurians. Therefore, on the day when the new consuls consulted the Senate concerning their bailiwicks and the condition of the state, the Senate decreed for both the Ligurians as their province. The consul Lepidus sought to veto this decree of the Senate: it was improper, he said, that both consuls should be shut up in the valleys of Liguria, while Marcus Fulvius and Gnaeus Manlius ruled for two years now, the one in Europe, the other in Asia, as if they were substitutes for Philip and Antiochus. If it were decided that armies should be in those lands, it was appropriate that consuls should command them, rather than private citizens" (*Si exercitus in his terris esse placeat, consules iis potius quam priuatos praeesse oportere*).

30 *TLL* s.v. "proconsul" = vol. 10, fasc. 2 (1998), p. 1542 line 17 – p. 1545 line 58 (Hadjú).

31 Claudius Quadrigarius fr. 57 FRHist = Gellius 2.2.13. Note that the mss of Gellius are by no means unanimous in their testimony for this paragraph: at both instances of the word's occurence, C uses the single lexeme *proconsul* but VPR employ the two words *pro consul* (presumably for *pro consule*).

32 *RS* no. 12, Cnidos Copy, column II, line 14, with the translation on p. 249.

33 *Lex Coloniae Genetivae* (*RS* no. 25) chapter 125, ll. 15–16: *iussu{q}ue C. Caesaris dict(atoris) co(n)s(ulis) proue | consule.*

34 *Supplementum epigraphicum Graecum* XVIII 555 = Sherk, *Roman Documents*, no. 61, line 12, a governor's edict from 27 BCE inscribed at Cyme: *Vinicius proconsul salutem dat magistratibus Cumas.* It is perhaps worth mentioning a related historical puzzle. Cassius Dio famously observes that emperors very often held office as consul and "were always called proconsul, whenever they were outside the *pomerium*" (53.17.4). That said, Augustus is only once named proconsul, on the peculiar *Tabula Paemeiobrigensis* of February 15 BCE, where, I observe, the orthography employed is *pro cos*, for *pro co(n)s(ule)* (l. 2). The matter received exemplary treatment, with an exhaustive rehearsal of the evidence, in the *editio princeps*: Alföldy, "Das neue Edikt," 192–5.

35 Suetonius *De viris illustribus* fr. 61 Reifferscheid: *Messala Corvinus primus praefectus urbis factus sexto die magistratu se abdicavit, incivilem potestatem esse contestans.* The fragment derives from Jerome's Chronicle, among the entries for the third year of the 188th Olympiad. See also Seneca *Apocolocyntosis* 10.2, where, in a moment laden with irony, Augustus says that he, like Messala, was ashamed of his power (*pudet imperii*); as well as Tacitus *Ann.* 6.11, where Messala resigns the *potestatem* "as if he didn't know how to exercise it." On the ideology of citizenly deportment see the classic study of Wallace-Hadrill, "Civilis Princeps."

36 Cicero *Leg. agr.* 1.19 and esp. 2.87–8.

37 Ando, "The Roman City."

38 One might read the late-second-century BCE Roman law on magisterial malfeasance, the *lex de repetundis*, in similar terms: it creates a mechanism to allow aliens access to Roman criminal courts, to render their cases justiciable, with the effect that they and their communities are at least contingently embraced by the domestic

machinery of the Roman state. On this point see Richardson, "The Purpose of the *lex Calpurnia de repetundis*," 10–11.

39 An absolutely exemplary essay with similar explanatory ambitions is Gotter, "Greek and Roman Concepts of Power."

40 For one excellent such attempt, rather different in emphasis than my own, see Bertrand, "Langue grecque et administration romaine."

41 A full study of these issues would record that one might translate πολιτεία into Latin as *res publica*: hence Cicero's use of *De re publica* for the title of his work inspired by Plato's *Republic*. One would then have to observe that *res publica* has no single correlate in Greek: even in a single text presumably translated by a single hand, such as the Greek translation of Augustus's *Res Gestae*, four different phrases are used to render *res publica* in Greek.

42 As one moves into the Byzantine period, *politeia* covers ever more of the territory of Latin *civitas*, part of a broad pattern of change – of Romanization – of Greek political thought: see Kaldellis, "Aristotle's *Politics* in Byzantium," 124, and idem, *The Byzantine Republic*. On the extension of the meaning of πόλις see Aelius Aristides *Or*. 26.75: when recruiting soldiers among alien populations, the Romans release them from their πατρίς (fatherland) and give them the Romans' πόλις as their own, and so make them into πολίται, fellow citizens.

43 On this point see Ando, "Imperial Identities." Though the issue reaches beyond the scope of the present work, I wish here to acknowledge the symbiotic aid given to fictive kinship in the self-understanding of Greek communities by their claims to shared *nomoi*, which constituted the biological community as simultaneously a moral one.

44 *Romanitas* first appears in Tertullian's *De pallio*, in discussing members of the Carthaginian elite who play at being Greek when they should act Roman. On this text see Ando, "Making Romans."

45 Aulus Postumius Albinus fr. 1b FRHist = Gellius 11.8.2–3. There are good reasons to believe that this text was written in Greek and translated into Latin, though it is not marked as such by Gellius. On this problem see S.J. Northwood in FRHist 1:187–8.

46 For a legally oriented study of the Latin right see Kremer, *Ius Latinum*.

47 That said, I respect the caution expressed by Roselaar, "Colonies and Processes," 528, to the effect that we have no literary evidence for the incorporation of persons who were neither Roman nor Latin in such colonies prior to the Second Punic War. Such evidence as we

do have (e.g., non-Roman, non-Latin onomastic evidence from inscriptions; formation of villages within colonial territory but outside the centuriated landscape) can generally not be dated so to require the incorporation of indigenes at foundation rather than the later migration of persons into colonial territory. Rarely does one get evidence like *ILS* 6753, an inscription from Aosta, referring to "Salassan non-citizen residents (*incolae*) who brought themselves into the colony from the beginning," to wit, at the colony's foundation in 25 BCE.

48 Cicero *Paradoxa Stoicorum* 29.

49 Cicero *Brut.* 74.258.

50 On this point, see also the conclusion to this volume, "Making Romans," on the phrase *pro cive gerere*, conducting oneself as if one were a citizen, as well as Ando, "Was Rome a *Polis*?" and *Imperial Ideology*. The latter works tell among others the story of how provincials came to self-identify as Roman, in consequence of which the term "Roman" ceased to suffice as a claim to the juridical quality of Roman citizenship. One had rather to specify, "I am a Roman citizen." On *patria* see Tacitus *Hist.* 5.5.2, where he describes converts to Judaism as repudiating their ancestral culture using the phrase *exuere patriam*, they "shed" or "stripped off their fatherland."

51 See, e.g., Julian *Digest* bk. 84 fr. 819 Lenel = *Dig.* 1.3.32.1: *Inveterata consuetudo pro lege non immerito custoditur, et hoc est ius quod dicitur moribus constitutum. nam cum ipsae leges nulla alia ex causa nos teneant, quam quod iudicio populi receptae sunt, merito et ea, quae sine ullo scripto populus probavit, tenebunt omnes: nam quid interest suffragio populus voluntatem suam declaret an rebus ipsis et factis? quare rectissime etiam illud receptum est, ut leges non solum suffragio legis latoris, sed etiam tacito consensu omnium per desuetudinem abrogentur.*

52 See also *Rep.* 1.41, a gathering of people might have an *oppidum* or *urbs*, but he singles out *populus* = *civitas* = *res publica* as a special type of collectivity.

53 I use the term "rightful order" to translate *ius* in an attempt to capture the distinction that Cicero seeks to draw between *lex*, on the one hand, which often means "statute" or "law" but can also mean "the law" more generally, and *ius*, on the other, which often means "the law" or "legal right" but can also refer to a legitimate normative order.

54 On this point see the brilliant essay of Moatti, "*Respublica* et droit dans la Rome républicaine," with further support at Ando, "Roman City," 114–15.

55 For an earlier use of sociare to a similar end, see Cicero *In Verrem* 2.5.167: *Homines tenues, obscuro loco nati, navigant, adeunt ad ea loca quae numquam antea viderunt, ubi neque noti esse iis quo venerunt, neque semper cum cognitoribus esse possunt. Hac una tamen fiducia civitatis non modo apud nostros magistratus, qui et legum et existimationis periculo continentur, neque apud civis solum Romanos,* qui et sermonis et iuris et multarum rerum societate iuncti sunt, *fore se tutos arbitrantur, sed, quocumque venerint, hanc sibi rem praesidio sperant futuram.*

56 As Bruce Lincoln has emphasized to me, not simply language and law, but also kinship and territory are purely human institutions, however much they misperceive and misrepresent themselves as facts of nature. These are, however, not essential themes of this volume, nor perhaps major constituents of a Roman social imaginary.

57 Nietzsche, "Über Wahrheit und Lüge im außermoralischen Sinn," 46–7: "Was ist also Wahrheit? Ein bewegliches Heer von Metaphern, Metonymien, Anthropomorphismen, kurz eine Summe von menschlichen Relationen, die, poetisch und rhetorisch gesteigert, übertragen, geschmückt wurden und die nach langem Gebrauch einem Volke fest, kanonisch und verbindlich dünken: die Wahrheiten sind Illusionen, von denen man vergessen hat, dass sie welche sind, Metaphern, die abgenutzt und sinnlich kraftlos geworden sind, Münzen, die ihr Bild verloren haben und nun als Metall, nicht mehr als Münzen, in Betracht kommen."

3 The Ontology of the Social

1 Cf. Ando, "The Edict of Serdica," distinguishing between imperial and civil modes of religious tolerance.

2 On this point see Ando, *Religion et Gouvernement*, chapter 3; see also idem, "Pluralism and Empire."

3 Ando, "Pluralism and Empire."

4 On *ius gentium* see Grosso, "Riflessioni su 'ius civile'"; Kaser, *Ius gentium*; Moatti, *Raison de Rome*, 163–5 and 287–98; and Ando, *Law, Language*, 19–36.

5 See, e.g., Gaius *Institutes* 1.52–5.

6 In addition to the passages quoted here see Varro *De gente populi Romani* fr. 21 Semi *apud* Servius *ad* Aen. 7.176 (*Maiores enim nostri sedentes epulabantur. quem morem a Laconibus habuerunt et Cretensibus, ut Varro docet in libris de gente populi Romani, in quibus dicit, quid a quaque taxerint gente per imitationem*); Cicero *Tusc.* 1.1; Diodorus 5.40.1 and 23.2.1; and Sallust 51.37–9 (from the speech of Caesar): *Maiores nostri, patres conscripti, neque consili neque audaciae umquam eguere; neque illis superbia obstabat quominus aliena instituta, si modo proba erant, imitarentur.*

7 The theme of comparison between the cultures that has achieved greater fame in modern literatures concerns citizenship, on which see Ando, "Making Romans."

8 On historical change within the Roman community as producing social and linguistic change see, e.g., Gellius 20.1, with Ando, "*Exemplum*, Analogy."

9 Cicero *Leg.* 1.17: *Natura enim iuris explicanda nobis est, eaque ab hominis repetenda natura; considerandae leges quibus civitates regi debeant; tum haec tractanda, quae composita sunt et descripta, iura et iussa populorum; in quibus ne nostri quidem populi latebunt quae vocantur iura civilia.*

10 Cicero *Rep.* 3.27 Powell; on this passage see Ando, "Cities, Citizenship."

11 Gaius *Ad legel duodecim tabularum* bk. 1 fr. 418 Lenel = *Dig.* 1.2.1.

12 Lucretius 5.1108–9 (*condere coeperunt urbis arcemque locare / praesidium reges ipsi sibi perfugiumque...*) and 5.1143–4 (*inde magistratum partim docuere creare / iuraque constituere, ut vellent legibus uti*).

13 Papinian *Definitiones* bk. 2 frag. 46 Lenel = *Dig.* 1.1.7.1.

14 *SEG* 39, no. 1180, cited here from the text and translation in Cottier et al., *Customs Law.*

15 Cicero *Rep.* 2.22; see also Polybius 6.47.

16 On Roman legal fictions see Ando, *Law, Language*, 1–18, and especially idem, "Fact, Fiction."

17 Tertullian *Quaestiones* bk. 1 fr. 5 Lenel = *Dig.* 1.3.27: *Ideo, quia antiquiores leges ad posteriores trahi usitatum est, semper quasi hoc legibus inesse credi oportet, ut ad eas quoque personas et ad eas res pertinerent, quae quandoque similes erunt.*

18 The treatment here tracks that in Ando, *Law, Language*, 1–8.

19 On "nature" in Roman law see the brilliant studies of Yan Thomas: "L'institution juridique de la nature"; "Imago naturae"; and "*Auctoritas legum non potest veritatem naturalem tollere.*"

20 On vegetal sacrifice see Scheid, *Quand faire, c'est croire*; on substitutionalism in respect to implements, see Ando, "Praesentia numinis. Part 2," discussing inter alia Festus s.v. struppi (472L): *Struppi vocantur in pulvinaribus <fasciculi> <de verbenis facti, qui pro de>orum capitibus ponuntur. . . . . . bem calo Antistius <Labeo . . . . . ma>gistratum publicum . . . .*; cf. Paul s.v. struppi (473L): *Struppi vocabantur in pulvinaribus fasciculi de verbenis facti, qui pro deorum capitibus ponebantur.*

21 Nock, "A Feature of Roman Religion," reprinted with translations of Greek and Latin texts in Ando, *Roman Religion*.

22 Adamik, "Temple Regulations from Furfo."

23 Ando, *The Matter of the Gods*, 10–15.

24 See also Livy 9.33.9: *quodque postremum iussisset id ius ratumque esset.* For different views as to the authenticity of this text see *FIRA* vol. 1, chapter II, "Lex XII Tabularum," XII.5; *RS* p. 721; and Oakley, *A Commentary on Livy*, 191.

25 Livy 9.33.8–9 and 9.34.6–7: *et quia, ubi duae contrariae leges sunt, semper antiquae obrogat noua.*

26 For an inquiry into these texts in light of scholarship on both ritual and law see Ando, *Law, Language*, 37–63.

27 In quoting Servius, I decline to distinguish between the sentences preserved in the shorter and longer "editions," the distinction being in this context irrelevant.

28 On these themes see also Ando, *Matter*, 1–18, and idem, "The ontology of religious institutions." The theme is now receiving some attention from specialists: see North, "Disguising Change," and Rüpke, "Historicisation of Religion."

29 See also Cicero *Flacc.* 69: *sua cuique civitati religio, Laeli, est, nostra nobis.* For an extended meditation on the institutionalization of religious pluralism in the high Roman empire, and in particular the similar conceptual apparatus used to describe and justify religious and legal pluralisms, see Ando, "Riten." For a congruent consideration of the emergent use of *religio* = religion in the context of late Republican empire see Giovanni Casadio's fine article "*Religio* vs. Religion," 308–20.

30 Varro *Antiquitates rerum divinarum* frr. 18, 36 and 37.

31 Varro *Antiquitates rerum divinarum* fr. 44: *censuerant, ne qui imperator fanum, quod in bello vovisset, prius dedicasset quam senatus probasset; ut contigit M. Aemilio, qui voverat Alburno deo.*

32 Roman literature regarding the ritual of *evocatio*, by which the Romans summoned forth the gods of hostile communities with the

offer of worship at Rome, is a case in point. Regardless of whether one credits Roman claims regarding the ritual's antiquity, or, like me, treats most such claims as antiquarian invention, the literature can nevertheless be read as instantiating a recognition of the social element in the divine. See Ando, *Matter*, 120–48.

33 I have myself attempted to analyse Roman accounts of diplomatic practice of the archaic and classical periods as organized around just these assumptions of cultural and institutional homology between parties, with the caveat that the political implications and degree of self-awareness involved in making such assumptions will naturally have varied from context to context: see Ando, "Aliens, Ambassadors," and *Law, Language*, 37–63.

Conclusion: Making Romans

1 On this distinction see esp. Hosking, "The Freudian Frontier," on which see Maier, *Among Empires*, 5.

2 On the emergence or, perhaps, the new salience of old forms of social differentiation in the aftermath of the Antonine Constitution see Bryen, "Reading the Citizenship Papyrus (P. Giss. I 40)"; see also Ando, *Critical Century*, 176–86.

3 These are obviously interpretive rather than absolute claims. For arguments tending in other directions, see, *exempli gratia*, Gruen, *Culture and National Identity*; Emma Dench, *From Barbarians to New Men*; Williams, *Beyond the Rubicon*; and Woolf, *Tales of the Barbarians*.

4 *Romanitas* is first attested c. 200 CE in Tertullian's *De pallio*, when Tertullian chides members of the Carthaginian elite for playing Greek and wearing fashionable Greek clothing, although they are Roman. As I have stressed elsewhere concerning the term *invisibilis* ("Praesentia numinis"), the form of the word *Romanitas* is so wholly regular that one cannot exclude the possiblity that it was used (or coined), and re-used (or re-coined) with some regularity.

5 TLL s.v. *fundus*. The term received an entry in Festus, though the abbreviation of the definition by Paul the Deacon displays no interest in the metaphorical relationship between the two usages: *Fundus dicitur ager, quod planus sit ad similitudinem fundi vasorum. Fundus quoque dicitur populus esse rei, quam alienat, hoc est auctor* (Festus s.v. *Fundus* 79L).

6 Mason Hammond, "Germana patria," 159–64 provides a clear treatment. See also Humbert, *Municipium*, 296–9, and Bispham,

From Asculum to Actium, 24–7, 87–9. Neither of these is interested in the metaphorical aspects of the language.

7 Ennius *Ann.* l. 157 Skutsch = l. 169 Vahlen[3] = Warmington Spuria no. 2, from [Censorinus], *De metris* in Keil, *Grammatici Latini*, 6:612: *Cives Romani tunc facti sunt Campani.*

8 Livy 9.43.22–4.

9 See, e.g., Cicero *De domo sua* 78, quoted above.

10 See, e.g., Cicero *Off.* 3.47; see also *Arch.* 11; Livy 32.2.6 and 34.42.5–6. Note, too, the diction of the emperor Claudius at *ILS* 206 *(tanquam cives Romani gesserunt egeruntque…)* and that of Livy at 34.42.6 (Latins had submitted their names to be colonists in Roman colonies and so had begun *se pro civibus Romanis ferrent*). A further use of the phrase has just come to light, in an historical context closely paralleling the case under Claudius, namely, an edict of Hadrian concerning elite soldiers who turn out not to have been citizens, though by law they could not have served in their units had their status been known. Hadrian grants them citizenship in such a way "that all those things that they did as if they were citizens, I confirm exactly as if they had been citizens when they began their military service" (*omnia, quae pro civibus Romanis gesserunt, proinde confirmo, quasi iam tunc, cum militare coeperunt, cives Romani fuissent)* (Eck, Pangerl and Weiss 2014). The language is also available in analogous contexts: according to Livy, in 199 BCE, representatives from the colony at Narnia came to Rome to complain that some non-citizens had moved to the colony and become "mixed in" (an idiom generally implying intermarriage) and hence, though not of the citizens' *genus, pro colonis se gerere*, "they were conducting themselves as colonists" (32.2.6–7).

11 I set aside here as outside the scope of the present book, in both substance and method, the enormously important and complicated question what the entailments of citizenship were understood to be, though this obviously bears on scope and significance of my argument.

12 On the myth of Romulus and its many forms and uses, see Wiseman, *Remus*, and Dench, *Romulus' Asylum*. On the retention of the past history of communities founded de novo as Roman towns see Ando, "Roman City," and esp. idem, "Mythistory."

13 On this point see Thomas, "La valeur des choses," as well as idem, "La construction de l'unité civique."

14 See Varro *Antiquitates rerum divinarum* fr. 44, quoted above in chapter 3 n. 31.

15 On this topic see Scheid, *Les dieux, l'État*, citing earlier bibliography. An English translation of this book will be published by the University of Pennsylvania Press under the title *The Gods, the State and the Individual: Reflections on Civic Religion at Rome.*

16 On this subject see Ando, "Religious Affiliation," citing earlier bibliography.

17 On doctrines of popular sovereignty over this period see Millar, *Rome, the Greek World, and the East*, 85–161.

18 Schrimm-Heins, "Gewißheit und Sicherheit," parts I and II. See also Kaufmann, *Sicherheit*.

19 Cicero *Pro Flacco* 15. It bears recalling that "fact" itself derives from a perfective participle: the fact has no existence in the world apart from the action that brings it into being; cf. German *Tatsache.*

Works Cited

Abbey, Ruth. "Back to Baczko." *European Journal of Political Theory* 5 (2006): 355–64.

Adamik, Tamás. "Temple Regulations from Furfo. CIL I^2 756)." In Heikki Solin, Martti Leiwo, and Hilla Halla-aho, eds., *Latin vulgaire – latin tardif VI*, 77–82. Hildesheim: Olms-Weidmann, 2003.

Alföldy, Geza. "Das Neue Edikt des Augustus aus El Bierzo in Hispanien." *Zeitschrift für Papyrologie und Epigraphik* 131 (2000): 177–205.

Ando, Clifford. "Aliens, Ambassadors and the Integrity of the Empire." *Law & History Review* 26 (2008): 491–519.

Ando, Clifford. "Diana on the Aventine." In Hubert Cancik and Jörg Rüpke, eds., *Die Religion des Imperium Romanum*, 99–113. Tübingen: Mohr Siebeck, 2009.

Ando, Clifford. "Die Riten der Anderen," translated by Gian Franco Chiai, Ralph Häussler and Christiane Kunst. *Mediterraneo Antico* 15 (2012): 31–50.

Ando, Clifford. "*Exemplum*, Analogy and Precedent in Roman law." In Michèle Lowrie and Susanne Lüdemann, eds., *Between Exemplarity and Singularity: Literature, Philosophy, Law*, 111–22. New York: Routledge, 2015.

Ando, Clifford. "Fact, Fiction and Social Reality in Roman Law." In Maksymilian del Mar and William Twining, eds., *Legal Fictions in Theory and Practice*, 295–323. Boston: Springer, 2015.

Ando, Clifford. "Imperial Identities." In Tim Whitmarsh, ed., *Local Knowledge and Microidentities in the Imperial Greek World*, 17–45. Cambridge: Cambridge University Press, 2010.

Ando, Clifford. "Law and the Landscape of Empire." In Stéphane Benoist and Anne Daguey-Gagey, eds., *Figures d'empire, fragments de mémoire: Pouvoirs (pratiques et discours, images et représentations), et identités (sociales et religeuses) dans le monde romain impérial. (Ier s. av. J.-C. - Ve s. ap. J.C.)*, 25–47. Paris: Presses Universitaires de Septentrion, 2011.

Ando, Clifford. "Making Romans: Democracy and Social Differentiation under Rome." In Myles Lavan, Richard Payne and John Weisweiler, eds. *Imperial Cosmopolitanisms. Global Identities and Imperial Cultures in Ancient Eurasia*, forthcoming.

Ando, Clifford. "Mythistory: The pre-Roman Past in Latin Late Antiquity." In Hartmut Leppin, ed., *Antike Mythologie in christlichen Kontexte der Spätantike – Bilde, Räume, Texte*, 205–18. Berlin: De Gruyter, 2015.

Ando, Clifford. "Pluralism and Empire, from Rome to Robert Cover." *Critical Analysis of Law: An International & Interdisciplinary Law Review* 1 (2014): 1–22.

Ando, Clifford. "Postscript: Cities, Citizenship and the Work of Empire." In Claudia Rapp and H.A. Drake, eds., *The Transformation of City and Citizenship in the Classical World: From the Fifth Century* BCE *to the Fifth Century* CE, 240–56. Cambridge: Cambridge University Press, 2013.

Ando, Clifford. "Praesentia Numinis. Part 1: The Invisibility of Gods in Roman Thought and Language." *Asdiwal* 5 (2010): 45–73.

Ando, Clifford. "Praesentia Numinis. Part 2: Objects in Roman Cult." *Asdiwal* 6 (2011): 57–69.

Ando, Clifford. "Religious Affiliation and Political Belonging from Caracalla to Theodosius." In progress.

Ando, Clifford. "The Edict of Serdica in Religious–Historical Perspective." In V. Vatchkova and D. Dmitrov, eds., *Serdica Edict. 311* AD*): Concepts and Realizations of the Idea of Religious Toleration*, 51–62. Sofia: Tangra TanNakRa, 2014.

Ando, Clifford. "The Ontology of Religious Institutions." *History of Religions* 50 (2010): 54–79.

Ando, Clifford. "The Origins and Import of Republican Constitutionalism." *Cardozo Law Review* 34 (2013): 917–35.

Ando, Clifford. "The Roman City in the Roman Period." In Stéphane Benoist, ed., *Rome, a City and its Empire in Perspective: The Impact of the Roman World through Fergus Millar's Research. Rome, une cité impériale en jeu: l'impact du monde romain selon Fergus Millar*, 109–24. Leiden: Brill, 2012.

Ando, Clifford. "Three Revolutions in Government." In Lucian Reinfandt, Stephan Prochazka, and Sven Tost, *Official*

Epistolography and the Languages of Power. Vienna: Verlag der Österreichischen Akademie der Wissenschaften, 2015.

Ando, Clifford. "Vergil's Italy: Ethnography and Politics in First-century Rome." In David S. Levene and Damien Nelis, eds., *Clio and the Poets: Augustan Poetry and the Traditions of Ancient Historiography*, 123–42. Leiden: E.J. Brill, 2002.

Ando, Clifford. "Was Rome a *Polis*?" *Classical Antiquity* 18 (1999): 5–34.

Ando, Clifford. *Imperial Ideology and Provincial Loyalty in the Roman Empire*. Berkeley: University of California Press, 2000.

Ando, Clifford. *Imperial Rome* AD *193 to 284: The Critical Century*. Edinburgh: Edinburgh University Press, 2012.

Ando, Clifford. *Law, Language and Empire in the Roman Tradition*. Philadelphia: The University of Pennsylvania Press, 2011.

Ando, Clifford. *Religion et Gouvernement dans l'Empire Romain*. Bibliothèque de l'École des Hautes Études. Turnhout: Brepols, 2014.

Ando, Clifford. *The Matter of the Gods*. Berkeley: University of California Press, 2008.

Ando, Clifford, ed. *Roman Religion*. Edinburgh: Edinburgh University Press, 2003.

Ari Z. Bryen. "Reading the Citizenship Papyrus. P. Giss. I 40." In Clifford Ando, ed., *Citizenship and Empire in Europe, 200–1900*. In progress.

Aubert, Jean-Jacques. "For Swap or Sale? The Roman Law of Barter." In Catherine Apicella, Marie-Laurence Haack, and François Lerouxel, eds., *Les affaires de Monsieur Andreau: Économie et société du monde romain*, 109–21. Bordeaux: Ausonius, 2014.

Barney, Stephen A., W.J. Lewis, J.A. Beach, and Oliver Berghof, trans. *The Etymologies of Isidore of Seville*. Cambridge: Cambridge University Press, 2006.

Béranger, Jean. *Principatus*. Publications de la Faculté des Lettres de l'Université de Lausanne, 20. Geneva: Droz, 1975.

Béranger, Jean. *Recherches sur l'aspect idéologique du principat*. Schweizerische Beiträge zur Altertumswissenschaft, 6. Basel: F. Reinhardt, 1953.

Berger, Adolf. *Encyclopedic Dictionary of Roman Law*. Transactions of the American Philosophical Society, n.s. Vol. 43, part 2. Philadelphia: American Philosophical Society, 1953.

Bertrand, Jean-Marie. "Langue grecque et administration romaine: de l'ἐπαρχεία τῶν Ῥωμαίων à l'ἐπαρχεία τῶν θρᾴκων." *Ktema* 7 (1982): 167–75.

Bispham, Edward. *From Asculum to Actium. The Municipalization of Italy from the Social War to Augustus*. Oxford: Oxford University Press, 2007.

Black, Max. *Models and Metaphor. Studies in Language and Philosophy*. Ithaca: Cornell University Press, 1962.

Breton, J.-F. *Inscriptions grecques et latines de la Syrie*, Vol. 8.3: *Les inscriptions forestières d'Hadrien dans le mont Liban*. Paris: Librairie orientaliste Paul Geuthner, 1980.

Brooke-Rose, Christine. *A Grammar of Metaphor*. London: Secker & Warburg, 1958.

Casadio, Giovanni. "*Religio* vs. Religion." In Jitse Dijkstra, Justin Koesen and Ymi Kuiper, eds., *Myths, Martyrs and Modernity. Studies in the History of Religion in Honour of Jan N. Bremmer*, 301–26. Leiden: Brill, 2010.

Castoriadis, Cornelius. *The Imaginary Institution of Society*. Cambridge: MIT Press, 1987.

Cavallar, Osavaldo, and Julius Kirshner, "Jews as Citizens in Late Medievial and Renaissance Italy: The Case of Isacco das Pisa." *Jewish History* 25 (2011): 269–318.

Chastagnol, André. "La législation sur les biens des villes au IVe siècle à la lumière d'une inscription d'Éphèse." In *VI Convegno internazionale dell'Accademia romanistica constantiniana*, 76–104. Perugia: 1986.

Clark, Robert Charles. "The Morphogenesis of Subchapter C: An Essay in Statutory Evolution and Reform." *Yale Law Journal* 87 (1977): 90–162.

Cottier, M., M.H. Crawford, C.V. Crowther, J.-L. Ferrary, B.M. Levick, O. Salomies, and M. Wörrle, eds. *The Customs Law of Asia*. Oxford: Oxford University Press, 2008.

Dench, Emma. *From Barbarians to New Men: Greek, Roman and Modern Perceptions of Peoples from the Central Apennines*. Oxford: Clarendon Press, 1995.

Dench, Emma. *Romulus' Asylum: Roman Identities from the Age of Alexander to the Age of Hadrian*. Oxford: Oxford University Press, 2005.

Eck, Werner, Andreas Pangerl, and Peter Weiss. "Edikt Hadrians für Prätorianer mit unsicherem römischen Bürgerrecht." *Zeitschrift für Papyrologie und Epigraphik* 189 (2014): 241–53.

Foucault, Michel. *The Order of Things. An Archaeology of the Human Sciences*. New York: Random House, 1970.

Gotter, Ulrich. "Cultural Differences and Cross-cultural Contact: Greek and Roman Concepts of Power." *Harvard Studies in Classical Philology* 104 (2008): 179–230.

Grosso, Giuseppe. "Riflessioni su 'ius civile,' 'ius gentium,' 'ius honorarium' nella dialettica fra tecnicismo-tradizionalismo giuridico e adeguazione allo svilippo economico e sociale in Roma." In *Studi in memoria di Guido Donatuti*, 1: 439–52. Milan: La Goliardica, 1973.

Gruen, Erich. *Culture and National Identity in Republican Rome.* Ithaca: Cornell University Press, 1992.

Hammond, Mason. "Germana patria." *Harvard Studies in Classical Philology* 60 (1951): 147–74.

Hosking, Geoffrey. "The Freudian Frontier." *Times Literary Supplement* no. 4797 (10 March 1995): 27.

Humbert, Michel. *Municipium et Civitas sine Suffragio. L'Organisation de la Conquête jusqu'à la Guerre Sociale.* Rome: École française de Rome, 1993.

Jakobson, Roman and Morris Halle, eds., *Fundamentals of Language.* 's-GravenHage: Mouton, 1956.

Kaldellis, Anthony. "Aristotle's *Politics* in Byzantium." In V. Syros, ed., *Well Begun Is Only Half Done: Tracing Aristotle's Political Ideas in Medieval Arabic, Syriac, Byzantine, Jewish, and Indo-Persian Sources*, 121–43. Tempe, AZ: Arizona State University Press, 2011.

Kaldellis, Anthony. *The Byzantine Republic: People and Power at New Rome.* Cambridge: Harvard University Press, 2014.

Kantor, Georgy. "*Siculus cum Siculo non eiusdem ciuitatis*: Litigation Between Citizens of Different Communities in the Verrines." *Cahiers du Centre Gustave Glotz* 19 (2010): 187–204.

Kaser, Max. *Ius gentium.* Cologne: Böhlau, 1993.

Kaufmann, Franz-Xaver. *Sicherheit als soziologisches und socialpolitisches Problem: Untersuchungen zu einer Wertidee hochdifferenzierter Gesellschaften.* Stuttgart: Ferdinand Enke Verlag, 1970.

Keil, Heinrich, ed., *Grammatici Latini*, Vol. VI, *Scriptores artis metricae.* Leipzig: 1874.

Kremer, David. *Ius Latinum. Le concept de droit latin sous la République et l'Empire.* Paris: De Boccard, 2006.

Lakoff, George, and Mark Turner. *More than Cool Reason: A Field Guide to Poetic Metaphor.* Chicago: University of Chicago Press, 1989.

Lavan, Myles. *Slaves to Rome. Paradigms of Empire in Roman Culture.* Cambridge: Cambridge University Press, 2013.

Lenski, Noel. *Failure of Empire. Valens and the Roman State in the Fourth Century* AD. Berkeley: University of California Press, 2002.

Maier, Charles S. *Among Empires. American Ascendancy and Its Predecessors.* Cambridge: Harvard University Press, 2006.

Millar, Fergus. *Rome, the Greek World, and the East,* Vol. 1: *The Roman Republic and the Augustan Revolution,* ed. Hannah M. Cotton and Guy M. Rogers. Chapel Hill: University of North Carolina Press, 2002.

Moatti, Claudia. "*Respublica* et droit dans la Rome républicaine." *Mélanges de l'École française de Rome, Moyen Âge* 113 (2001): 811–37.

Moatti, Claudia. *La raison de Rome.* Paris: Éditions du Seuil, 1997.

Nerlich, Brigitte and David D. Clarke. "Synecdoche as a Cognitive and Communicative Strategy." In Andreas Blank and Peter Koch, eds., *Historical Semantics and Cognition,* 197–213. New York: De Gruyter, 1999.

Nietzsche, Friedrich. "Über Wahrheit und Lüge im außermoralischen Sinn." In Walter Kaufmann, ed. and trans., *The Portable Nietzsche.* New York: Viking, 1954.

Nock, A.D. "A Feature of Roman Religion." *Harvard Theological Review* 32 (1939): 83–96.

North, John. "Disguising Change in the First Century." In Jörg Rüpke, ed., *The Individual in the Religions of the Ancient Mediterranean,* 58–84. Oxford: Oxford University Press, 2013.

Oakley, S.P. *A Commentary on Livy Books VI–X,* Vol. 2: Books VII and VIII. Oxford: Oxford University Press, 1998.

Pocock, J.G.A. *The Machiavellian Moment. Florentine Political Thought and the Atlantic Republican Tradition.* Princeton: Princeton University Press, 1975.

Richardson, J.S. "The Roman Mind and the Power of Fiction." In L. Ayres, ed., *The Passionate Intellect: Essays Presented to Professor I.G. Kidd,* 117–30. New Brunswick, NJ: Transaction, 1995.

Richardson, John. "The Purpose of the *lex Calpurnia de repetundis.*" *Journal of Roman Studies* 77 (1987): 1–12.

Richardson, John. *The Language of Empire. Rome and the Idea of Empire from the Third Century* CE *to the Second Century* AD. Cambridge: Cambridge University Press, 2008.

Roselaar, Saskia. "Colonies and Processes of Integration in the Roman Republic." *Mélanges de l'École française de Rome, Séries Antiquité* 123 (2011): 527–55.

Rüpke, Jörg. "Do Gods have a History? Historicisation of Religion in the Roman Republic." *History of Religions* 53 (2014): 246–68.

Scheid, John. *Les dieux, l'État et l'individu. La religion civique dans la Rome antique.* Paris: Seuil, 2013.

Scheid, John. *Quand faire, c'est croire. Les rites sacrificiels des Romains.* Paris: Aubier, 2005.

Schrimm-Heins, Andrea. "Gewißheit und Sicherheit: Geschichte und Bedeutungswandel der Begriffe 'certitudo' und 'securitas' (Teil I)." *Archiv für Begriffsgeschichte* 34 (1991): 123–213.

Schrimm-Heins, Andrea. "Gewißheit und Sicherheit: Geschichte und Bedeutungswandel der Begriffe 'certitudo' und 'securitas' (Teil II)." *Archiv für Begriffsgeschichte* 35 (1992): 115–213.

Shaw, Brent. "Autonomy and Tribute: Mountain and Plain in Mauretania Tingitana." In P. Baduel, ed., *Desert et montagne: hommage à Jean Dresch. Revue de l'Occident Musulman et de la Méditeranée* 41–2 (1986): 66–89.

Sherk, R.K., ed. *Roman Documents from the Greek East: Senatus Consulta and Epistulae to the Death of Augustus.* Baltimore: Johns Hopkins University Press, 1969.

Smith, J.Z. *Drudgery Divine.* Chicago: The University of Chicago Press, 1990.

Stini, Frank. *Plenum exiliis mare: Untersuchungen zum Exil in der römischen Kaiserzeit.* Geographica Historica 27. Stuttgart: Franz Steiner Verlag, 2011.

Taylor, Charles. "The Dynamics of Democratic Exclusion." *Journal of Democracy* 9.4 (1998): 143–56.

Taylor, Charles. *Modern Social Imaginaries.* Durham, NC: Duke University Press, 2004.

Taylor, Lily Ross. *The Voting Districts of the Roman Republic: The Thirty-five Urban and Rural Tribes.* Rome: American Academy in Rome, 1960.

Thomas, Yan. "*Auctoritas legum non potest veritatem naturalem tollere.* Rechtsfiktion und Natur bei den Kommentatoren des Mittelalters." In François Kervégan and Heinz Mohnhaupt, eds., *Recht zwischen Natur und Geschichte = Le droit entre nature et histoire,* 1–32. Frankfurt: Klostermann, 1997.

Thomas, Yan. "Imago naturae. Note sur l'institutionnalité de la nature à Rome." In *Théologie et droit dans la science politique de l'État moderne,* 201–27. Rome: École française de Rome, 1991.

Thomas, Yan. "L'institution juridique de la nature. Remarques sur la casuistique du droit naturel à Rome." *Revue d'histoire des Facultés de droit et de la science juridique* 5 (1988): 103–28.

Thomas, Yan. "La construction de l'unité civique. Choses publiques, choses communes, choses n'appartenant à personne et représentation." *Mélanges de l'École française de Rome, Moyen Âge* 114 (2002): 7–39.

Thomas, Yan. "La valeur des choses. Le droit romain hors la religion." *Annales, Histoire, Sciences sociales* 6 (2002): 1431–62.

Thomas, Yan. *"Origine" et "commune patrie." Étude de droit public romain. (89 av. J.-C. – 212 ap. J.C.).* CÉFR 221. Rome: École Française de Rome, 1996.

Turner, Mark. "Figure." In Albert N. Katz et al., eds., *Figurative Language and Thought*, 44–87. New York: Oxford University Press, 1998.

van Hook, Larue. *The Metaphorical Terminology of Greek Rhetoric and Literary Criticism.* Dissertation: The University of Chicago, 1905.

Vico, Giambattista. *Institutiones Oratoriae.* Ed. Giuliano Crifò. Naples: Istituto Suor Orsola Benincasa, 1989.

Vico, Giambattista. *The Art of Rhetoric* (*Institutiones Oratoriae, 1711–1743*). Trans. Giorgio A. Pinton and Arthur W. Shippee. Amsterdam and Atlanta, GA: Rodopi, 1996.

Vico, Giambattista. *La Scienza nuova.* Ed. Palo Rossi. Milan: Rizzoli, 1959.

Vico, Giambattista. *The New Science*, 3rd edition, 1744. Trans. Thomas Goddard Bergin and Max Harold Fisch. Ithaca: Cornell University Press, 1948.

Wallace-Hadrill, Andrew. "Civilis Princeps: Between Citizen and King." *Journal of Roman Studies* 72 (1982): 32–48.

Weil, Patrick. *The Sovereign Citizen: Denaturalization and the Origins of the American Republic.* Philadelphia: The University of Pennsylvania Press, 2012.

Williams, J.H.C. *Beyond the Rubicon. Romans and Gauls in Republican Italy.* Oxford: Oxford University Press, 2001.

Wiseman, T.P. *Remus: A Roman Myth.* Cambridge: Cambridge University Press, 1995.

Woolf, Greg. *Tales of the Barbarians: Ethnography and Empire in the Roman West.* Malden, MA: Wiley-Blackwell, 2011.

Index

www.ingramcontent.com/pod-product-compliance
Lightning Source LLC
LaVergne TN
LVHW090200080826
844660LV00013B/888/J
9781442650176